7

D1756940

Falling Down

✖ Controversies

Series editors: Stevie Simkin and Julian Petley

Controversies is a series comprising individual studies of controversial films from the late 1960s to the present day, encompassing classic, contemporary Hollywood, cult and world cinema. Each volume provides an in-depth study analysing the various stages of each film's production, distribution, classification and reception, assessing both its impact at the time of its release and its subsequent legacy.

Also published

Shaun Kimber, *Henry: Portrait of a Serial Killer*
Neal King, *The Passion of the Christ*
Peter Krämer, *A Clockwork Orange*
Gabrielle Murray, *Bad Boy Bubby*
Stevie Simkin, *Basic Instinct*
Stevie Simkin, *Straw Dogs*

Forthcoming

Julian Petley, *Crash*
Lucy Burke, *The Idiots*
Tim Palmer, *Irreversible*

'The *Controversies* series is a valuable contribution to the ongoing debate about what limits – if any – should be placed on cinema when it comes to the depiction and discussion of extreme subject matter. Sober, balanced and insightful where much debate on these matters has been hysterical, one-sided and unhelpful, these books should help us get a perspective on some of the thorniest films in the history of cinema.'
Kim Newman, novelist, critic and broadcaster

Falling Down

Jude Davies

First published 2013 by
PALGRAVE MACMILLAN

Palgrave Macmillan in the UK is an imprint of Macmillan Publishers Limited, registered in England, company number 785998, of Houndmills, Basingstoke, Hampshire RG21 6XS.

Palgrave Macmillan in the US is a division of St Martin's Press LLC, 175 Fifth Avenue, New York, NY 10010.

Palgrave Macmillan is the global academic imprint of the above companies and has companies and representatives throughout the world.

Palgrave® and Macmillan® are registered trademarks in the United States, the United Kingdom, Europe and other countries

ISBN: 978–0–230–32134–2

This book is printed on paper suitable for recycling and made from fully managed and sustained forest sources. Logging, pulping and manufacturing processes are expected to conform to the environmental regulations of the country of origin.

A catalogue record for this book is available from the British Library.

A catalog record for this book is available from the Library of Congress.

Printed in China

Contents

Part 1: Making *Falling Down*

Part 2: The Controversy

Part 3: The 'Crisis of White Masculinity'

Part 4: Reading *Falling Down*

Part 5: The Legacy of *Falling Down*

Appendices..125

List of Figures

Acknowledgements

All screen captures taken from *Falling Down,* Region 2 DVD, Alcor Films/ Canal+/ Regency Enterprises/Warner Bros., except for figure 12, taken from *Disclosure,* Region 2 DVD, Warner Bros./Baltimore Pictures/Constant c Productions, 1994.

Alasdair Spark and Fran Mason were there at the beginning, an unofficial excursion to the cinema by the Department of American Studies at the University of Winchester, and have remained perceptive and generous interlocutors. Thanks are also due to colleagues past and present at Winchester who have encouraged or stimulated the work culminating in this book, especially Andrew Blake, Martin Pumphrey, Inga Bryden, Steve Allen, Leighton Grist, Laura Hubner, and Tony Dean.

Liam Kennedy and John Carlos Rowe have been particularly wise and knowledgeable sparring partners. Other intellectual debts are made clear in the pages that follow. By far the greatest such debt is to Carol R. Smith, who first demonstrated to me the important conjunction of film with identity politics in the 1990s, and whose ideas continue to inform this book.

I would also like to thank the readers and editors at *Screen* and the *Journal of Gender Studies* for their appreciation and suggestions on my early attempts to get a critical purchase on *Falling Down*. Further support and enthusiasm at critical points came from George McKay and Ann Kaloski-Naylor.

Thanks also to Denise Hanrahan Wells for sharing her insight into gender in 1990s American film, and to all those students who have discussed *Falling Down* intelligently on the module 'Identity in American Film' at the University of Winchester.

On this project specifically I owe a large debt of gratitude to Stevie Simkin and Julian Petley, for valuable advice as much as for acknowledging the need for this book. I am also very grateful to Juliet Williams for her excellent work as a research assistant, funded under the University of Winchester Research Apprenticeship Programme. Thanks also to Simon Matthews for loaning research materials.

My deepest thanks to Carol for holding the fort while I've been tapping away – now it's your turn. And to Rosa, who shines like the sun.

This book is dedicated to Margaret Leah and to Stephen Davies, my parents.

✖ Introduction

Some films are born controversial, some films achieve controversial status, and some films have controversy thrust upon them.[1] *Falling Down* exemplifies all three.

The courting of controversy had become central to Michael Douglas's professional persona well before he lent his iconic presence and box office appeal to a screenplay that had reportedly been rejected by every major studio. As he put it in an interview promoting *Falling Down*

> I respect controversy. My film career life has been made up of controversy. I go back to *One Flew Over the Cuckoo's Nest* and the psychiatric community was very upset with us. *The China Syndrome* – the nuclear energy [industry] was very upset. *Fatal Attraction* – single women were very upset. *Wall Street* – anybody involved in the banking or investment community was very upset. *Black Rain* – police officers; and some people accused us of being racists in *Black Rain* although the Japanese nominated the picture for best foreign film. *War of the Roses* – divorcées, you know. So it's been a constant ... And so I think it's a compliment when there's a reaction. That means that somebody has felt something. Now, if you can do that, and in the case of *Falling Down*, leave the theatre and still have a morsel of thought, or controversy, that's healthy. (Schumacher, 1993/2009)

Even by Douglas's consistently provocative standards (and he does not even mention what had been his most controversial movie so far, 1991's *Basic Instinct*, perhaps because it might be hard to categorise neatly as 'respectable' and 'healthy') *Falling Down* would upset many people. Both the star and the director Joel Schumacher explicitly intended that the film would 'strike a nerve', that is, that it would inflame sensitivities that normally remain below the surface of mainstream culture. As the reactions of many viewers and critics would testify, it did strike a nerve. But not necessarily the same nerve. The production of the film was overtaken by events that redefined and complicated its provocation. In particular, towards the end of April 1992, location shooting had to be suspended because much of South Central Los Angeles had been set on fire. Triggered by the acquittal on 29 April of four white police officers accused of beating the black motorist Rodney King the 'L.A. riots' or 'uprising' was the worst outbreak of urban disorder in the United States since the 1960s. After six days, 51 people were dead, and 700 business had been destroyed, causing damage estimated to cost $1bn.

Set in a territorialised Los Angeles utterly lacking civility, *Falling Down* seemed to mimic the riots by depicting the angry violence of a central protagonist (D-Fens, the unemployed defence worker played by Michael Douglas), who has lost any faith in economic and judicial institutions. The targeting of a Korean shopkeeper in an early scene paralleled the attacks on Korean-run businesses that were widely reported as being focal points of the disturbances. Still, as Douglas, Schumacher, and producer Arnold Kopelson were at pains to point out, these were unintended coincidences. *Falling Down* might have echoed the freewheeling violence of the riots, but in one crucial respect it was out of touch. The sense of racial injustice that triggered the riots was given its cinematic apotheosis elsewhere, in the opening titles of Spike Lee's *Malcolm X* (1992), which intercut video footage of the beating of Rodney King, with the stars and stripes in flames. All of which only highlighted the racial whiteness of the central protagonist of *Falling Down*, albeit that this particular white guy half realises that he has more in common with people of colour than he had ever imagined. If *Falling Down* was born controversial, the riots thrust upon it a controversy that its makers had not anticipated.

Successive waves of controversy broke over the film after its release on 26 February 1993. Early reviewers compared D-Fens to the New York 'subway vigilante' Bernhard Goetz, who had shot four alleged muggers in December 1984, and worried that the film might inspire similar acts of violence. Reports described audiences whooping in enjoyment at the violent retribution dished out in the film to the Korean shopkeeper and Latino gang members. Screenings were picketed by Asian American groups led by the Korean American Coalition, and further protests came from the National Center for Career Change, who feared that the psychotic character portrayed by Douglas would stigmatise jobless defence workers. Los Angeles was reportedly 'in uproar' (Reinhold, 1993) over the movie's portrayal of the city as a territorialised battleground, and the *Los Angeles Times* published a series of articles in the city's defence. By the end of March the controversies ignited by the film had gone national. The subject of television shows and newspaper articles, D-Fens stared aggressively through his broken glasses from the cover of *Newsweek*, the epitome of what the magazine called 'white male paranoia'. The accompanying article crystallised what was becoming a common view of the film: in a nutshell, that it legitimated a growing resentment among certain white men towards a multicultural America which no longer granted the privileges formerly accruing through masculinity and white racial identity.

This book tries to make sense of *Falling Down* in all its incoherence and ambiguity. More than this, it assesses the historical and cultural significance not only of the film itself but also of the various debates and conflicts which it provoked. In other words, it constitutes as an object of study the controversies surrounding the film. The argument here coincides with that of Kendall R. Phillips, who urges that controversy itself deserves more attention as 'a vital stage that falls in between the feeling of offence and the legal machinations of censorship' (2008, p. xv); a stage too often neglected by certain academic approaches to controversial films.

Falling Down and much of its coverage in print media and on television belonged to what might be called a 'controversy culture', emerging in the 1990s alongside the proliferation of media channels on television and, later, the world wide web. Breaking down boundaries between current affairs and entertainment, investigative journalism and expert commentary, controversy culture has since become ubiquitous on television and online. For some, this has generated anxieties that the values of responsible enquiry and interrogation have been subjugated to the demands of mere entertainment. Others have celebrated the dynamism of 'postmodern' cultural forms, seeing them as more open and democratic. This book rejects both these positions. As it makes clear, readings of *Falling Down* were from the first also interventions in far-reaching debates over gendered and racial identity, as well as sites of political conflict and negotiation.

As a preliminary, a detailed synopsis provides both a straightforward account of *Falling Down*, and indicates those aspects of production design, shooting and editing, *mise-en-scène*, and production, which are particularly influential in determining its cinematic effects and its wider cultural significance. Part 1 then charts the making of the film, from the roots of Ebbe Roe Smith's original screenplay to the production process, during which it was reshaped by Schumacher and Douglas amongst others. Part 2 traces the history of the *Falling Down* controversy as it unfolded in the American media after the film's release.

Part 3 moves outwards from the *Falling Down* controversy in popular media to the wider contexts of the 'culture wars' of the early 1990s USA, the resonant term used to describe the political reaction to the qualified success of identity politics in the 1970s and 1980s. Specifically, it examines the various meanings of the so-called crisis of white masculinity historically and in terms of their impact on critical theory. The approach taken here lies at the intersection of debates over film violence with the new understanding of cinematic representations of identity that emerged in the 1990s as academics responded to Hollywood's engagement with identity politics. In the context of debates over film violence, the central question about *Falling Down* can be put relatively simply: Does the film legitimate (white male) violence, or pathologise it? However, as will be seen, the answer to this question is complicated by the ways in which *Falling Down* encourages audiences to make multiple and split identifications, with and/or against D-Fens, his ex-wife Beth, and Prendergast, the cop who tracks his path across Los Angeles and eventually kills him.

It is this purposeful ambiguity that makes the controversy over *Falling Down* more than just historically significant. Paradoxically, it also makes it necessary to supplement analysis of the film itself with an understanding of the wider context of the struggles over identity that informed the film-makers' vision and the frameworks of interpretation used by audiences. Had the film been identifiable with a particular position in the culture wars, it might have become notorious, but it would not have sparked the debates that it did. What made *Falling Down* deeply controversial is what continues to make it fascinating: the blurring between its sense of a nation in crisis, a loss of civility that affects everybody, and a specific identity – that of the white male – that is in crisis. This ambiguity is crystallised in the ways that the film presents D-Fens as both a universal figure – a 'consumer' and an 'American' – and as a white unemployed man, a member of an identity group that for the first time in American history had acquired the status of victim, and required group advocacy.

Throughout this discussion of wider historical and theoretical contexts, the film itself remains a touchstone. In particular, Part 4 focuses sharply on important scenes from *Falling Down*, in the context of historical and critical debates over identity and representation. The analysis of these key scenes pays particular attention to the viewing positions that they seem to privilege, the viewing pleasures offered, the depiction of racial and gendered identity, and reports of research into audiences' reactions.

Taken together, Parts 3 and 4 argue in detail that *Falling Down* represents a pivotal moment in the trajectory of white masculinity in the United States, and, by implication, in the West more generally; one caught between outworn forms of a bogus universalism, and emerging forms that are still coalescing 20 years later. *Falling Down* is in this sense the cultural condensation of the crisis of white masculinity elaborated at length in Susan Faludi's *Stiffed: The Betrayal of the Modern Man* (1999). This is to evoke the pivotal nature of *Falling Down*'s depiction of white masculinity, but more than this, and more interestingly, it also frames the film's depiction of identity and anger with respect to the political opposition between multiculturalism and approaches that seek to negate or ignore difference. What is ultimately at stake is not simply a debate over progressive or reactionary forms of masculinity, or even over gender and social justice, but a wider question concerning the possibility of separating the liberating elements of Western democratic traditions from their patriarchal and racial hierarchies. Part 5 brings these considerations together in assessing the historical importance of *Falling Down* and its legacy for both cinematic and television depictions of 'race'[2] and gender. There we assess how what Douglas called *Falling Down*'s 'morsel of thought, of controversy' continues to relate to the debates over identity that bubble through cultural and political life on both sides of the Atlantic and in the rest of the world.

✖ Synopsis

This detailed synopsis is intended both as a summary of the film in the traditional sense, and for reference in conjunction with the analysis of specific scenes in Part 4.

A Note on Names

The central protagonist of *Falling Down*, played by Michael Douglas, is known by several different names or nicknames during the film. To his family he is William or 'Bill' Foster, while to the police tracking a white guy across Los Angeles he becomes D-Fens, after his personalised car licence plate (the name used in the film's closing credits), and then GI Joe, after he dons an army jacket from a military surplus store. These names not only register shifts in his roles, his appearance, and his behaviour; they also function to map and to emphasise specific poles of identification or conversely, alienation, for audiences. What follows attempts to render this aspect of the film, but it should be borne in mind that such judgements are more than usually subjective.

Falling Down opens in the unbearable heat of a rush-hour traffic jam. A white guy (Michael Douglas) in his late 30s, wearing a white shirt and tie, glasses and a buzz cut, becomes increasingly frustrated and eventually gets out of his car and abandons it. As the sound of a police helicopter is heard in the background, he takes a briefcase with him, telling bystanders that he is 'going home'. The car is pushed off the freeway by a motorcycle cop and two men caught up in the traffic jam, a travelling salesman, and a balding, moustached man in his 50s (Robert Duvall) who introduces himself as Detective Prendergast from the downtown Robbery division, on his last day before retirement. Throughout the scene the camera has lingered on signs of various sorts, including bumper (fender) stickers, car window decals, road furniture, and dot matrix signs warning of delays due to roadworks. Two signs arrest Prendergast's attention: the abandoned car's personalised licence plate 'D-FENS'; and a huge billboard on the side of the freeway advertising 'Hawaiian Tropic' sunscreen, which shows a tanned young woman of Caucasian appearance with the slogan 'White Is For Laundry'. A graffiti artist has added a punky, Kilroy-like figure, but instead of peering over a wall, the cartoon man is apparently falling down between the woman's breasts, with a voice bubble shouting 'HELP!!'

In Venice Beach a woman carrying groceries (Beth, played by Barbara Hershey), her daughter (Adele, played by Joey Hope Singer), and Labrador dog run to their house – a small ranch house painted white like the picket fence outside – to answer the ringing telephone. But when Beth picks up, the line goes dead.

Figure 1:   White is for laundry.

On the other end of the telephone was the white guy who abandoned the car with the D-FENS plate. He puts down the receiver of a payphone and examines his remaining change. There is not enough for another call so he crosses the road to a Mom and Pop store. Here on the other side of the freeway embankment, the environment is unmistakeably that of the economically depressed inner city. There is graffiti everywhere, and in the background a homeless woman tends her bags. Inside the store, D-Fens asks the Korean shopkeeper (Michael Paul Chan), who is unshaven, and frequently scratches his stomach, for change. The shopkeeper insists, somewhat aggressively, that he buy something. D-Fens chooses a can of 'classic' coca cola from the refrigerator, which he holds to his head to cool down. In heavily accented English, the shopkeeper asks for 85 cents, which, as D-Fens points out, would not leave enough change for the telephone. As the tension between the two rises, the shopkeeper pulls out a baseball bat from under the counter. D-Fens seizes the bat and uses it to smash up several displays of goods, declaring that he is 'standing up for my rights as a consumer' and 'rolling back prices to 1965'. At length, he puts a dollar bill into the till to pay for the coke and takes 50 cents change. The shopkeeper cowers in a corner as D-Fens leaves, carrying the can of coca cola, the baseball bat, and his briefcase.

From this point on scenes alternate between the progress of D-Fens across Los Angeles towards Venice Beach, the police department's tracking of the mayhem he causes, and Beth's increasingly anxious day at home. In the next scene Prendergast has arrived in his office, which is large and open-plan, with a City of Los Angeles crest on one wall. As part of the high jinks accompanying his last day at work, a colleague has filled his desk drawer with used cat litter. Prendergast is systematically belittled as a 'desk jockey' by his fellow detectives, who include white males Lydecker (D.W. Moffet) and Graham (Macon McCalman); Brian, a Japanese American (Steve Park); Jones, a black woman (Kimberly Scott); and Sanchez, a Latino (Richard Montoya). Only Sandra, or Sandy, Torres (Rachel Ticotin) is friendly and supportive. Prendergast draws out from the cat litter a framed photograph of a two-year old girl, and looks at it.

In Venice, Beth is filling a blue plastic water pistol she has just bought for Adele, while she makes a telephone call.

Back in graffiti-land, D-Fens stands at a payphone, listening impatiently to the busy tone. He walks up a small hillock and is followed by two men (Agustin Rodriguez and Eddie Frias) whose tattoos, demeanour, and accents identify them as members of a Latino street gang.

Prendergast is called by his wife Amanda (Tuesday Weld), who is nervous about his welfare on this last day. He reassures her and they both sing the nursery rhyme 'London Bridge is Falling Down' to the musical mechanism inside a snow globe, a reference to the historical London landmark now situated in Lake Havasu, Arizona, which is to be their retirement destination. His reassurances to her imply that he has taken a desk job, and early retirement, in order to assuage her extreme anxiety – an explanation that Prendergast will later confirm to Sandra Torres.

In the urban wasteland, with skyscrapers in the background, D-Fens examines a hole in the sole of his shoe. He is approached by the two gang members, who menace him and accuse him of loitering and trespassing on their property. He responds aggressively at first, then tries to be conciliatory, but they demand his briefcase as a toll and one pulls out a switchblade. D-Fens attacks them with the baseball bat, grabs the knife, and bellows 'I'm going home…Clear the path you motherfuckers, I'm going home'. He tries unsuccessfully to operate the switchblade, and pockets it.

In the police station, Prendergast signs a form and hands back his gun. Detective Brian asks him to interview Mr Lee, the Korean shopkeeper, who describes the attack on his store and the loss of the baseball bat. Brian resents Prendergast's expectation that he, a Japanese American, can translate between English and Korean.

At another phone booth, upon which stickers in Spanish are prominently displayed, D-Fens finally gets through and tells Beth that he's 'coming home' for Adele's birthday. She reminds him that he does not pay child support and that their house is not his home, and threatens to call the police. While D-Fens is on the phone he is spotted by the gang members, who are driving down the street accompanied by two other young Latino men and a young woman, Angie (Karina Arroyave). In spite of Angie's pleas for caution, they eject her from the car and drive by D-Fens spraying automatic gunfire. Broken glass flies all over the place, several bystanders are injured, possibly killed, but D-Fens is miraculously unharmed (a mural of Jesus is seen nearby). The driver loses control of the car, and it crashes. D-Fens approaches, picks up one of the gang's guns and levels it 'Dirty Harry' style. Having missed with a first shot, he takes careful aim but at the last moment shifts angle and shoots the gang member in the leg. He calmly picks up the bag of weapons and crosses the street. Angie runs past him in the opposite direction, distraught at the violent death of her friends.

Prendergast is debriefed by his boss Captain Yardley (Raymond J. Barry) in the latter's office. Yardley struts his own physical prowess and again demeans Prendergast. It transpires that Prendergast and his wife had a daughter, who died when two years old.

Between scenes of D-Fens's encounters with a construction worker who blocks his way, and a homeless man who asks him for money, Beth tries with difficulty to explain his propensity for violence to two police officers who have evidently responded to her call. She describes an exclusion order which prevents her ex-husband coming close to her house, but cannot remember whether the distance stipulated is a 100 feet or a 100 yards.

At the police station, Detectives Jones and Sanchez interview Angie, while Prendergast watches through a two-way mirror. He suspects that Mr Lee's assailant is the same as the white guy that Angie describes, but Sanchez proprietorially warns him off the case.

D-Fens enters a fast food restaurant branded 'Whammyburger' and tries to order from the breakfast menu, which has just expired. In the ensuing confrontation with crew member Sheila (Dedee Pfeiffer) and manager Rick (Brent Hinkley), he pulls an Uzi from his bag of guns and accidentally shoots into the ceiling. Eventually he receives a 'poor, squashed thing' of a burger, which he compares invidiously with the photographs on display, addressing the burger bar's customers. In response to his question 'What's wrong with this picture?', a young African American boy raises his hand.

Before there can be an exchange between the boy and D-Fens, the film cuts to Prendergast and Sandra, who go to lunch at a Mexican restaurant. Sandra tackles him about leaving the police force early to please his wife, but their friendly, intimate conversation is interrupted rudely by Lydecker with news of the Whammyburger incident.

A high-angle shot picks out an African American in white shirt, dark trousers and a tie (Vondie Curtis-Hall), who is protesting outside a bank. He carries a placard with the words 'Not Economically Viable', a phrase used by the bank to deny him a loan, which he implies was in reality due to racism. Across the street, D-Fens buys for three dollars a snow globe with a unicorn inside, as a birthday present for his daughter. He watches as the protester is arrested and taken away in a police car. They exchange a meaningful look, and the protester urges 'Don't forget me'. D-Fens nods, turns and watches the police car drive away, as long trumpet phrases are heard on the soundtrack, reminiscent of Miles Davis's classic style.

The police officers leave Beth's house. D-Fens tries to phone again, and then shoots up the phone booth to stop an impatient man using it. Mrs Prendergast phones Prendergast again to give him a list of shopping to do on his way home.

D-Fens walks into a military surplus store looking for hiking boots to replace his worn-out shoes. The owner, Nick (Frederic Forrest), who has heard about the Whammyburger incident on his police scanner, greets him warmly. In the police station, Angie confirms to Prendergast that the white guy has taken the gang's bag of guns, and in a reverie Prendergast sees his daughter, her eyes open but evidently either dead or dying, on a hospital gurney. Back in the surplus store, Nick abuses and threatens two gay men browsing through the racks of clothes. When Sandra arrives looking for the white guy, Nick helps to hide D-Fens and subjects her verbally to sexual harassment, which she bats off confidently, as she has done before with Lydecker. After she has left, Nick takes D-Fens into the back room of the store. He proudly shows off items of Nazi memorabilia, and gives D-Fens a disposable rocket launcher to help him with his presumed vigilante activities. He then reacts violently when D-Fens objects to his racism and homophobia. Nick smashes the unicorn snow globe and carries out an assault on D-Fens with sexual and racist overtones. D-Fens falls and cracks one lens of his eyeglasses, but manages to get the switchblade out of his pocket and stab Nick in the shoulder. Then, as their reflections are caught together in a mirror, D-Fens shoots the neo-Nazi dead.

At the station, the ridiculing of Prendergast continues, led by Captain Yardley, who attacks him for not swearing as well as for his perceived cowardice, and the process is amplified by Jones and Sanchez. All three reject his theory that the incident in the store, the drive-by shooting, and the Whammyburger episode all feature the same white guy. Only Sandra Torres is convinced. Leaving his desk for, apparently, the first time in years, Prendergast sets off with Sandra to interview Mr Lee.

The film cuts between the back room of the surplus store and Beth's house in Venice. D-Fens calls and tells Beth that, like the astronauts on the ill-fated Apollo mission, he has 'passed the point of no return'.

As Prendergast arrives at Mr Lee's shop, he recognises the billboard advertising sunscreen and realises that the white guy they are pursuing was the man that he saw abandoning his car on the freeway: D-Fens.

The latter continues his journey, now wearing an army jacket from the surplus store. Encountering another traffic jam, he punches a man in a car who has been verbally abusing a female driver, and then browbeats a construction worker over the closure of a section of highway. In a scene played for comedy, he operates the rocket launcher with the help of a black youth who thinks it is part of a movie. This causes an explosion in the middle of the roadworks, scattering frightened construction workers.

Prendergast and Sandra arrive at the address they have obtained via D-Fens's car licence number, and interview his mother. Prendergast charms

Mrs Foster, and she unwittingly confirms their view of her son Bill as a potentially violent man. Prendergast finds a box of drawing instruments, a photograph of Bill with Elizabeth and Adele, and a wedding ring. Sandra uses her police radio to find out that Bill was fired from Notec, a defence contractor, over a month ago. Meanwhile, the man himself, still dressed as GI Joe, scales the fence surrounding the Altmore Country Club. In a blackly comic scene, he confronts two elderly golfers who resent his presence in their territory. He criticises the expropriation of land where children should be playing, and ridicules the golfers' 'stupid little carts', shooting at one which ends up sliding into a pond. The more aggressive golfer becomes so agitated that he aggravates a heart condition, and dies.

GI Joe next turns up, having cut himself on some barbed wire, in the garden of an expensive house, where he comes upon the groundskeeper and his family, who are using the swimming pool illicitly. The parents explain that the house belongs to a plastic surgeon. Hearing the sounds of a police pursuit, they assume that GI Joe is looking to take hostages, but he abruptly switches mood and behaviour. Now the broken father Bill Foster, he takes the hand of one of the children tenderly, and explains to them all that he has lost his job: 'I'm obsolete. I'm not economically viable. I can't even support my own kid.' He reminisces about his past married life, and weeps.

A police officer leaves the Venice house, while Prendergast pieces together the white guy's movements on a large wall map of Los Angeles.

Getting closer, Beth's ex-husband calls from a payphone surrounded by hippie paraphernalia, ads for yoga, and a faux-Native American bird sculpture. He complains that their favourite ice-cream parlour has been turned into 'some kind of Southwest American New Age thing'. Beth and Adele escape out of the side of the house as Bill bursts in at the front. They run to Venice pier.

Torres and Prendergast discuss the two latest incidents involving GI Joe, and Sandra finds an address in Venice for Beth Foster-Travino on the police computer. This is predicted by Prendergast on the basis of the white guy's path which he has tracked across Los Angeles, although he quips 'Where else would an Italian move to?'

GI Joe stays inside the house, sadly but calmly watching an old home video of Adele's second birthday. Prendergast and Torres decide to get to Beth's house as soon as possible, but they are interrupted when Amanda Prendergast phones again. Prendergast finally cracks and orders her to 'shut up', prepare his dinner, and to leave the skin on the chicken. She knuckles down immediately; it is almost as if she has craved his assertion of domestic authority all along – just as viewers have been eager for him to stand up for himself, at least in the workplace. Prendergast and Torres are then momentarily detained by the cake and the stripper that Detective Lydecker has organised for his farewell party. When Lydecker insults Prendergast's wife, Prendergast punches him.

In Beth's house, Bill watches himself in the home video becoming increasingly impatient and hectoring towards his daughter. As he realises that Beth and Adele have gone to the pier, Prendergast and Torres arrive. Torres goes to the back of the house, and Prendergast reaches for his gun, only to realise that he had handed it back earlier in the day. Instantly, offscreen, Torres shouts 'Freeze' and we hear a gunshot. Prendergast enters the house and finds Torres in the back yard, wounded although not fatally. GI Joe runs to the pier, and Prendergast takes Torres's pistol before setting off after him.

On Venice Pier the film builds to its climax. While Beth's back is turned as she buys pretzels, Adele recognises 'Daddy' running towards them. Bill, who wears a deranged expression for the first time in the film, forcibly embraces and kisses Beth. He puts down his gun to talk to Adele, hugging her and crying. Beth tells him that he is sick and needs help. Prendergast arrives and Bill picks up the gun again. The pace slows markedly for a while. Trying to calm Bill down, Prendergast talks about pollution in the sea, his upcoming retirement, his wife, and the death of his child due to 'infant death syndrome'. He begins to usurp Bill's paternal status by giving a tub of popcorn to Adele. She offers it to Bill, who again puts down his gun. This enables Beth to kick the gun away and throw it into the sea. She and Adele run to safety leaving the two white guys to shoot it out.

'I'm the bad guy?' asks Bill. 'How did that happen? I did everything they told me to. Did you know I used to build missiles?' Prendergast tells him that they lie to everybody and the only thing that makes him special is his little girl. Bill claims that he still has a gun, and challenges Prendergast to a 'showdown between the sheriff and the bad guy'. They draw, and Bill is hit. As he falls backwards we see that his only weapon was Adele's toy, the blue water pistol. Prendergast wipes something from his moustache. 'I would have got you', says Bill, before toppling backwards over the railings into the ocean. Long trumpet phrases are heard, like the sounds that had accompanied the African American protester's exit.

Prendergast returns to Beth's house, en route telling Captain Yardley 'Fuck you' as the latter is being interviewed live on television. Torres is being treated by medics and will recover. Prendergast advises Beth on how to explain things to Adele, whose birthday guests are arriving, and then sits beside the young girl on the front step. 'My name is mud', he tells her, 'or at least it will be, when my wife finds out I'm still a cop'. The camera pans back, and then follows two police officers into the house, where the old home video is still playing. The camera closes in on these blurred images and sounds of the Foster family in happier times, until they are cut off abruptly by a black screen.

✖ P<small>ART</small> 1

MAKING *FALLING DOWN*

The Principals: Ebbe Roe Smith, Michael Douglas, and Joel Schumacher

Like any other movie, *Falling Down* was a collaborative production, subject to institutional constraints, and shaped by the general social, economic, and cultural context of its moment. It is worth noting the influence of cinematographer Andrzej Bartkowiak and production designer Barbara Ling on the look and feel of the film, as well as James Newton Howard's music, and some powerful supporting performances, especially by Robert Duvall and Frederic Forrest. With these qualifications, the making of the film can be traced largely through the contributions of its three principals: screenwriter Ebbe Roe Smith, star Michael Douglas, and director Joel Schumacher.

Born in Los Angeles but by the early 1990s resident in New York, Ebbe Roe Smith's career had been primarily as a character actor, mainly playing villains in films such as *The Big Easy* (1986) and *Turner & Hooch* (1989), and in 1980s television shows such as *Hill Street Blues* and *T. J.*

Figure 2:   Screenwriter Ebbe Roe Smith (centre), with the motorcycle cop and Prendergast.

Hooker. He has a cameo in the opening scene of *Falling Down* as the travelling salesman who helps to push D-Fens's car off the freeway.

Having written several plays for small-scale theatre productions, Smith was unknown as a screenwriter when he submitted *Falling Down* to producer Arnold Kopelson. The project was initially a hard sell, according to some accounts being rejected by every major studio (Salisbury, 1993, p. 77; Parker, 2011, p. 327). At one point Kopelson was about to sell the property 'watered down and cheaply' (Parker, 2011, p. 327) to a cable television company, said to be Home Box Office (HBO) (Weinraub, 1992; Appelo, 1993). (It is intriguing to speculate on what an HBO production might have made of the troubling figure of D-Fens.) A turning point came when the script was shown to Michael Douglas, whose track record for making films that were both financially successful and dealt with controversial issues was second to none. Douglas's enthusiasm and participation attracted studio support in the form of Warner Brothers, who assigned a budget of between $25 and $30 million. This included a reported $8 million for the star (Dougan, 2001, p. 201), a major slice of the total, but only just over half the fee Douglas had commanded for his previous film, *Basic Instinct*. It was Douglas's participation that made the project financially viable, and it was also Douglas who was responsible for bringing in director Joel Schumacher. A self-described liberal moviemaker, Schumacher came from a blue-collar background in New York that contrasts sharply with Douglas's status as the scion of Hollywood legend Kirk. Nevertheless the two had been friends for two decades, with a closeness that came from being forged before the major successes that enabled Douglas to step out from the shadow of his famous father. The pair had worked together most recently on *Flatliners* (1990), which Douglas co-produced. Both, as well as Kopelson, were experienced, high-profile Hollywood figures in comparison to Smith, but it was Douglas's iconic presence that overshadowed the others. For audiences, *Falling Down* was primarily the latest in a long line of provocative, controversial movies in which Douglas had starred or had produced. Not only does his performance contribute in a major way to the impact of *Falling Down*, but his star persona decisively shaped the context in which audiences viewed the film, and it continues to do so. Comparatively few people will have bought a ticket to *Falling Down* in order to see a Joel Schumacher film. Nevertheless, as will be seen, the director's contribution to *Falling Down* went well beyond his consummately professional shaping of the movie.

'The "Headline" Type of Screen Story'

Looking back on *Falling Down,* Joel Schumacher described his intention as trying 'to give a face and a soul to that Six O'Clock News story we see all the time, the one about the seemingly ordinary man ... who snaps suddenly' (Salisbury, 1993, p. 77). The idea of a film that plays like a news item drew upon a longstanding Hollywood tradition, one that was, coincidentally, particularly associated with Warner Bros, the studio that produced *Falling Down* and that had made its name in the early 1930s with crime movies and prison pictures that resembled the news stories of Depression-era America. Epitomised by *The Public Enemy* (1931) and scores of B-movies, these films featured actors such as James Cagney and John Garfield playing characters who were both heroes and antiheroes, blue-collar men pushed to violent extremes by desperate situations. In a widely quoted 1932 article for *The Hollywood Reporter*, Darryl Zanuck, then Head of Production at Warner Bros, described the studio's specialty as the '"headline" type of screen story' adding that 'Somewhere in its makeup, it must have the punch and smash that would entitle it to be a headline on the front page of any successful metropolitan daily' (cited in Talbot, 2012, p. 35). Generated by the need to compensate for Warners' lack of capital and star names compared with other studios, the strategy resulted in films that, though not affiliated with realist aesthetics, dramatised the realities of the Great Depression more directly than did the rest of Hollywood.

In many respects, the appeal of 'the "headline" type of screen story' was the same 60 years later. Topicality pulled in free publicity and still gave legitimacy to sensational 'punch and smash'. The billing of *Falling Down* as 'a tale of urban reality' and 'the adventures of an ordinary man at war with the everyday world' highlighted a direct updating of the newsworthy qualities articulated by Zanuck. *Falling Down* also recapitulated the dualistic depiction of male (anti)heroism that loomed large in Production Code-era movies, which overtly condemned their criminal protagonists, yet spent much of the narrative soliciting sympathy for them. There are particularly strong parallels between D-Fens and Tom Powers (James Cagney), the central character of *The Public Enemy*, both in their escalating use of violence and in the tragic homecoming that constitutes the climax of both films. D-Fens's 'I'm the bad guy' resonates with the wounded Powers's 'I ain't so tough'. In addition to these generic precedents, it was, fittingly, a news story that directly inspired Smith's screenplay. In his most detailed account of the screenplay's genesis, Smith describes being fascinated by a *Los Angeles Times* article on 'a trucker who flipped out on a freeway and started ramming people' (Smith, 2012).[3] Disregarding what he saw as incidentals, for example the fact that the truck driver had been taking drugs, Smith seems to have treated the news report as an invitation to a fantasy of empowerment, imagining the trucker asking himself 'Why am I bothering with these little cars?' This he combined with another more mundane and personal fantasy of simply escaping a traffic jam by leaving one's car on the freeway, to produce the initial premise of the film. As Smith recalls, he then added the notion of 'a man walking in a straight line across a city...in a certain state of mind', an idea drawn from an earlier one-man play. This provided both the settings, areas that most middle-class people normally would drive past at speed, and many of the incidents of the film, which Smith describes as deriving directly from his own experiences of everyday life in Los Angeles. Subsequently he filled in the identity of the central protagonist, again following a newspaper report concerning workers in the defence industry who had been laid off due to the end of the Cold War in 1989. The interest here lay in the irony of individuals having succeeded at their work, in having ensured the security of the United

States by helping to bring about the fall of the Soviet Union, only to make themselves obsolete by that very success.

It is clear from this brief summary how Smith's original screenplay sowed some, though by no means all, of the seeds for the *Falling Down* controversy. Evidently the blend of news report and fantasy, which both assured topicality and proved to have potent audience appeal, was there from the beginning. So too is the *donné* of the film, the traffic jam as an emblem of modernity at its most dysfunctional, frustration at which crosses boundaries of class, 'race' and gender, yet is also customarily associated with certain large American cities, and with Los Angeles in particular. Present too is the central ideological provocation of the film: the protagonist's angry, extreme response to a widely shared set of frustrations and disappointments. Smith's identification of the central protagonist with unemployed defence workers also links the plight of a specific group of people to a questioning of American national identity, evoking the apparent betrayal of such workers against the wider uncertainty over national identity, which was the darker side of post-Cold War triumphalism. As Schumacher would recall while promoting the film's release in the United Kingdom, 'I felt that Ebbe had struck a nerve, that he had gone right to some kind of nerve in the culture, but I knew that it had political and economic and social ramifications. It was a movie that had something to say, and wasn't some kind of polemic, soapboxy thing. It was darkly funny with that everyday *insanity* to it' (Salisbury, 1993, p. 77). From the first, then, Smith's screenplay had hit upon D-Fens as, in the phrase used to promote the film 'An ordinary man at war with the everyday world'. But Schumacher was also well aware of the particular racial and gendered identity of the screenplay's protagonist, suggesting that Smith's script contained 'a monstrous anger that actually reflected the views of a wide cross-section of American society'. If this suggests a partial sympathy with D-Fens's anger, even while confessing it monstrous, Schumacher would also distance himself from it in very clear terms: 'It was a script that dealt with racist, bigoted people who were angry that all they had worked for was disappearing' (Parker, 2011, p. 328). It was precisely these complexities and contradictions that would make the film controversial, as they reflected the intensely conflicted status of white masculinity and its representation in American culture during the 1990s. The precise 'political and economic and social ramifications' of this particular depiction of white male anger were worked out in successive revisions to Smith's script.

From Screenplay to Script: Normalising D-Fens

The screenplay in which Ebbe Roe Smith had interested Arnold Kopelson, and which subsequently attracted Michael Douglas, was both more tightly defined by the thriller genre, and more extreme in its depiction of white rage, than was the movie they eventually made. As Smith puts it, 'the original [screenplay] was a darker film'. The central protagonist was 'more trigger-happy in it' (Smith, 2012), yet also, like his predecessor Paul Kersey (Charles Bronson) in the *Death Wish* films, survived to fight another day. In successive rewritings of the script, which went on until at least 11 May 1992, D-Fens's violence was softened or reduced in several significant ways, and the narrative changed so that Prendergast kills him rather than talks him down. Sequences in which D-Fens shot directly and recklessly into the gang members' car, and shot dead Rick, the manager of the Whammyburger restaurant, were removed. The scene in the garden of the plastic surgeon's house was radically changed, substituting the groundskeeper's family for the plastic surgeon and his wife, who, as early scripts had it, D-Fens forced to expose her breasts, in order sarcastically to applaud the work done to enhance them. In addition, the scene on the golf course where D-Fens confronts wealthy white men was interpolated, with the intention, as Roe Smith puts it, 'to broaden the social range' of his antagonists (Smith, 2012). Other revisions reduced the emphasis on the theme of D-Fens's dysfunctional relationships with women. In addition to the changes to the scene in the grounds of the plastic surgeon's house, a scene was cut in which D-Fens had encountered a woman and child, and, in pursuit of non-sexual

intimacy, got into bed with the woman. The script had originally ended
in the apartment of D-Fens's ex-wife, with the Prendergast figure able to
negotiate a peaceful resolution with him. The effect of these changes is not
only to make D-Fens more sympathetic, but also to direct attention away
from male–female relationships and to emphasise instead the male–male
encounter culminating in the extended face-off between D-Fens and
Prendergast as 'the sheriff and the bad guy'.

Smith attributes these changes to 'the studio' and its attempt to make
D-Fens a more sympathetic figure who would retain the empathy of the
audience for longer. He also, generously, suggests that they made the film
more engaging and successful (Smith, 2012). Schumacher's contribution in
particular was crucial. 'Originally', according to John Parker, 'the script had
D-Fens going wild very quickly; but the director slowed the action, to let
the tension build to achieve audience identification, so the audience could
see there was some justification in everything that D-Fens did' (Parker 2011,
p. 330). Whatever the exact motivation or provenance of these changes, it is
clear that they have intensified the controversy surrounding the film simply by
creating ambiguity around D-Fens and his anger. Was he being offered as an
everyman or an 'angry white male'? When could or should viewers empathise
with his frustration and share his release? And at what point, or points, should
we become alienated? It was not just that *Falling Down* raised these issues –
it was that the film would both engage and confuse audiences by soliciting
sympathy for a violent man who was, according to Douglas, 'nuts' before the
film narrative even starts (Schumacher, 1993/2009). On the film's release,
certain critics pointed to this fundamental ambivalence surrounding D-Fens
as a fatal flaw. For example, Hal Hinson accused the film-makers of pulling 'a
nifty little switcheroo' by first turning 'their Everyman into an avenging angel',
and then pointing 'a condemning finger at us for rooting for him'. The late
revelation that D-Fens had a history of violent behaviour means that 'instead
of being a movie about an average guy who snaps, *Falling Down* is about a nut
case pretending to be an average guy who snaps'. 'That no one seems to have
noticed the difference between these two states of mind', according to Hinson,

'is the movie's gravest problem' (1993). Hinson's apparent resentment at being manipulated, and his sense of D-Fens as polarising masculinity into extremes of 'average guy' and 'nut case', raise serious questions which will be examined further in Parts 2 and 3. Still, it is worth asking what is at stake in the implicit demand for movies to be clear and consistent in their eliciting of sympathy or identification. For example, it could be argued that audiences' capacities for mixed and ambivalent identifications are a prerequisite for cinema's capacity to deal with complex issues – Warner Bros gangster movies of the 1930s being a particular case in point. If the portrayal of the white male (anti)hero in *Falling Down* required audiences to make split and ambivalent identifications, these were only intensified by the screenplay's fusion of a revenge-thriller plotline with a state-of-the-nation polemic. This would seem, at least, what Schumacher was getting at when he described the 'everyday insanity' of the script. Either way, if the roots of the controversy over *Falling Down* lay in the generic hybridity of Smith's original conceit, its power was redoubled by the subsequent revisions to the script, and by Schumacher's deliberate building of audience identification with D-Fens. And taken further still by the provocative star persona projected by Michael Douglas.

Michael Douglas's Career of Controversy

Michael Douglas had imbued himself with controversy ever since he produced the film of Ken Kesey's countercultural novel *One Flew over the Cuckoo's Nest* in 1975, which antagonised not only the psychiatric community but also Kesey himself, who regarded the shooting script as a travesty of his work, and sued. By the time of *Falling Down*, the courting of controversy had become fundamental to Douglas's star persona, generating not only box office appeal but also underwriting his integrity and seriousness as a film-maker. As Douglas's biographer John Parker puts it, 'the movies in which he chose to appear were, by and large, a reflection of current social issues; they were always controversial and invariably pushed the

subject-matter to permissible extremes. That's what made him a superstar'
(2011, p. 323). In short, the trajectory, which began with his producer's
role in bringing Kesey's provocative novel to the screen, intensified by *The
China Syndrome* (1979), *Fatal Attraction* (1987), and *Basic Instinct*, prepared
audiences for the 'Michael Douglas movie' as a kind of Rorschach test of
some divisive contemporary popular issue.

    Falling Down continued this trajectory, which would peak with
Disclosure in 1994. Aside from the value of this strategy, both in marketing
terms and in staking a claim to cultural seriousness, up to and including
Basic Instinct the courting of controversy also provided a means for Douglas
to negotiate the perennial problem faced by actors in managing public
perceptions of their investment in specific roles. However, *Falling Down*
was produced and released into an atmosphere in which Douglas was losing
control of the boundaries between his personal and professional life. On
17 September 1992, while the film was in post-production, Douglas checked
into the Sierra Tucson Clinic, Arizona, for a month-long programme of
'curative guidance', reportedly to treat addictions to drugs, alcohol, and sex
(Peretz, 2010; Parker, 2011, p. 321). The revelations and rumours concerning
Douglas's personal life provided a burst of publicity for the previous year's
Basic Instinct, a film whose plot dynamic pivots on the inability of Douglas's
character to control his sexual desire for Catherine Tramell (Sharon Stone).
The same did not quite happen in terms of creating pre-publicity for
Falling Down. In part this was due to the overt importance of 'race', which,
as will be seen in Part 2, made the resentments simmering in Douglas's
character much more controversial. But it was also due to a major shift in
the depiction of gender, away from the highly sexualised themes focused by
the pre-feminist figure of the *femme fatale* and towards more overtly post-
feminist representations of the weakening and regeneration of male power.

    According to Parker, Douglas was drawn to *Falling Down* precisely
because it represented an opportunity to play a powerful loner male, in
contrast to the 'fall guy for women', a character reacting to female dominance,
which he considered himself to have played in the succession of movies back

from *Basic Instinct* and *Fatal Attraction* to *Romancing the Stone* (1984), *The Jewel of the Nile* (1985) and *The War of the Roses* (2011, p. 326). The prominent female characters in *Basic Instinct* (Stone) and *Fatal Attraction* (Glenn Close) had attracted much criticism as targets in a 'backlash', in Susan Faludi's terms, against feminism and gay liberation (Faludi, 1999, pp. 140–150; see also Simkin, 2013). But in *Falling Down*, D-Fens's ex-wife Beth remains a minor character, defined exclusively in terms of motherhood, the classic endangered female whose main contribution is to kick away D-Fens's gun at a crucial moment. This took Douglas's courting of controversy onto another level, potentially offering up his own struggle to be centre-stage as a parallel or mirror to D-Fens's feelings of displacement and anger.

The Riots/Uprising

At 3 pm on 29 April 1992, a jury in Simi Valley near Los Angeles pronounced a verdict of not guilty in the trial of four white Los Angeles Police Department officers charged with beating the African American motorist Rodney King. The charges related to an incident on 3 March 1991, following a high speed pursuit of King's car in Los Angeles County. (Unusually, the state court granted the defence's request for a change of venue to the mostly white suburb in neighbouring Ventura County, on the grounds of the widespread publicity surrounding the case.) An amateur video recording of the attack taken by George Holliday, which was widely televised, had seemed to offer conclusive evidence of guilt, and in a later federal trial the police officers would be convicted of violating King's civil rights.

Within hours of the acquittal, disturbances started in South Central Los Angeles and Koreatown. First, a kind of protest was made by stealing malt liquor from a store; then, at the intersection of Florence and Normandie Streets, young men began throwing rocks and bottles at police. That night local shops and stores, many of them owned by Korean Americans, were burned and looted. In another incident that was videotaped and widely and repeatedly screened on television, a white truck driver named Reginald Denny was pulled from his cab at a street corner and beaten almost to death with pieces of concrete. Amid increasing violence in South Central Los Angeles and Koreatown, and rising anxiety throughout the city, a state of emergency was declared and the National Guard called out. Six days of rioting followed, at the end of which 2,383 people had been injured, 8,000 arrested, and 51 killed. Over 700 businesses were burned, causing losses estimated at $1bn (Bergesen and Herman, 1998, p. 39). This was the most violent civil disturbance in the United States for over a century, more wrenching even than the 'race riots' of the 1960s, and comparable in scale with the draft riots in New York in 1863. One small side-effect was that location shooting of *Falling Down* had to be suspended, as police and troops from the National Guard had sealed off much of South Central Los Angeles.

While the immediate trigger for the riots is obvious, commentators and sociologists have debated the reasons exasperation and resentment at the apparent racism of the King verdict was manifested in such extreme and sustained violence, much of it directed against Korean immigrants. Some have cited the existence of a mostly black economic underclass (Callinicos, 1992), others the LAPD's long history of racist brutality and territoriality (Herbert, 1996), and yet others, tensions following the migration of Latinos and Koreans into areas previously dominated by African Americans (Bergesen and Herman, 1998). But what does seem clear is that, like George Holliday's videotape of the Rodney King beating, the riots themselves became, as Robert Gooding-Williams has explained, a news event of spectacular force that engaged powerful, if conflicting, feelings about 'race' and ethnicity (see Gooding-Williams, 1993). For Susan Faludi, that media event was 'staged with significant production assistance from the Los Angeles Police Department', who, shortly after the initial incidents, 'notified the media of a police action in progress, then promptly pulled out of the area' (1999, p. 480).

Michael Douglas and Ebbe Roe Smith later testified to their shock at seeing the city in flames (Douglas, 2009; Smith, 2012). What they seem to have felt was at stake here, beyond fears for their personal safety, was a breakdown of civic values, with people who may indeed have had a just grievance simply giving up on the judicial and legal systems and taking the law into their own hands. Still, the disturbances had relatively little effect on the actual production of *Falling Down*, merely delaying filming for a few days. Producer Arnold Kopelson would later recall that the opportunity to take and incorporate footage from the riots was rejected, as the film-makers were well aware of the distinction between the individual anger of their hero and the poverty and racial strife that characterised the uprising. Nevertheless, he admitted that the riots 'left an imprint' on the film (Weinraub, 1992). Not least due to the parallels with D-Fens's attack on Mr Lee's store, the uprising created a volatile context for audiences and critics, and *Falling Down* was forever linked with traumatic real-world violence and civil disorder. By February 1993 that trauma had become a powerful media event, manifested repeatedly on television via grainy videotape taken from helicopter-borne cameras, its causes investigated and debated extensively. Primed by Douglas's previous films, audiences expected that *Falling Down* would offer some kind of political or social insight: not at all a usual expectation of the thriller genre. So it was that the film came to be seen as topical, but also, to many, as spectacularly misdirected, obsessing about a *white* problem that represented only a fraction of the manifold issues facing Los Angeles and the United States more generally, if not pointedly evading the experiences of minority racial and ethnic groups, African Americans, Latinos, and Korean Americans, that were at the centre of the 1992 disturbances.

A few weeks before its release, *Falling Down* was previewed in Santa Monica. According to Parker, 'the location was carefully selected, a little pocket of middle-class WASPness in Greater Los Angeles ... virtually devoid of multiracial tensions, and no guns or gangs' (2011, p. 332). No doubt the aim was to canvass opinion that would be indicative of the film's reception nationally, but the balkanised logic of the movie itself makes it impossible not to draw a parallel between this appeal to a very white, middle-class 'jury' and the displacement to Simi Valley of the trial of Rodney King's assailants.

✖ Part 2

THE CONTROVERSY

Overview: Striking Several Nerves

Falling Down's release on 26 February 1993 provoked a series of debates in popular media, especially in print journalism. The central issue was always in some way D-Fens's violence in relation to the social landscape that the film portrays as fractured along lines of 'race', gender, and class. That core controversy took on a dynamic of its own as it unfolded in different contexts throughout the following month. A number of the early film reviews attacked *Falling Down* on moral and ethical grounds, reiterating the anxieties over film violence that had previously been raised by vigilante thrillers such as *Death Wish* (1974) and its sequels. Over the next three weeks, the film's nationwide popularity, coupled with reports of pickets and protests at screenings in Los Angeles, prompted further coverage outside of the film review pages. The most common theme here was the film's representation of minority groups such as Korean Americans, and of Los Angeles itself, which were scrutinised in the tradition of contesting the 'negative images' that had for decades been an important strategy in identity politics. By the end of March, focus had shifted decisively to the figure of D-Fens as an icon of 'white male paranoia', embodying conflicts over 'race' and gender on the national stage. Whereas D-Fens had at first been compared with vigilante figures in earlier thrillers and recent American history, he was eventually viewed less as a genre figure, and more as the embodiment of a new sociological and political phenomenon, the 'angry white male'.

First Reviews: Thrillers and the Morality of Film Violence

Generally the province of specialist film critics, opening weekend reviews considered *Falling Down* primarily within a cinematic context. Most regarded the film as something of an anomaly within the urban thriller genre. Critical assessments covered a wide spectrum, some regarding it as being triumphantly original, others seeing it as a flawed film but an interesting take on contemporary life, whilst a substantial minority excoriated it as morally objectionable and a cinematic failure. At one end of the scale Mick LaSalle wrote in the *San Francisco Chronicle* that the film 'violates formula' to such a degree that it is 'one of the great mistakes of 1993, a film too good and too original to win any Oscars but one bound to be remembered in years to come as a true and ironic statement about our life and time'.[4] Vincent Canby (1993) took a similar view in the *New York Times*, calling *Falling Down* 'the most interesting all-out commercial American film of the year' and likening its effect to a 'Rorschach test to expose the secrets of those who watch it'. At the other extreme were the minority of early reviews that accused the film-makers of irresponsibly indulging audiences' violent fantasies. For them *Falling Down* was 'determined to glibly escape the moral consequences of the vicarious white-rampage fantasies to which it caters' (Jay Carr in the *Boston Globe*); D-Fens's 'adventures would be offensive if you could take them seriously' (*TV Guide*); the film was 'a distasteful jumble that stirs up the worst instincts of its audience' (*Christian Science Monitor*), or 'an intellectually sloppy, rebellious working-man adventure film that is little more than a set piece for Michael Douglas playing out a revenge-of-the-nerds fantasy' (Siskel, 1993, chapter 1). In these negative readings, Schumacher and Douglas were accused of 'having their cake and eating it' in gaining sympathy for D-Fens as the victim of anti-social behaviour and then apparently validating his violent responses.

Such negative reviews drew upon well-worn, if still powerful, anxieties over the ethics of film violence, which emphasised *Falling Down*'s generic affiliation with certain 1970s thrillers. David Ansen viewed D-Fens as 'Howard ("I'm mad as hell") Beale in *Network* crossed with Charles Bronson in *Death Wish*, *Taxi Driver*'s Travis Bickle and the real-life Bernie Goetz' (Ansen, 1993, p. 80); a combination repeated, minus *Taxi Driver*, in Hal Hinson's *Washington Post* review. Sidney Lumet's *Network* (1976) does provide an interesting parallel in that it dramatises the on-air breakdown of a news anchor played by Peter Finch, suggesting links between the protagonists' 'falling down' and wider social and cultural issues. Very different resonances were brought up by references to the 'subway vigilante' Bernhard Goetz, who had become nationally famous, or infamous, after shooting four young African Americans on the New York subway in December 1984, fearing that they were about to mug him. In fact, Goetz's career in the public eye offers significant parallels with that of D-Fens in the film. Fears over public safety fuelled by New York's high crime rate had initially made Goetz a popular figure, although this was partially reversed by revelations about his history of using firearms and racist language. D-Fens was often described in similar terms, as first gaining audience identification as he faces every day, 'universal' frustrations, and then losing it as his history of violence is revealed. Still, it was another movie, Michael Winner's *Death Wish*, which in the early 1970s had defined the vigilante film and become notorious for playing to audiences' violent revenge fantasies, that was the most significant touchstone in these early reviews.[5]

When film critics such as Ansen, Hinson, and Turan compared D-Fens to Goetz and the protagonists of 1970s vigilante thrillers they were staking out the initial positions in a controversy that would soon spill beyond the context of American cinema. It is therefore worth pausing to consider the scope and limits of these early comparisons in purely cinematic terms. The sense of D-Fens as a composite thriller (anti)hero is indicative of audience expectations about the character's role and perhaps of the kinds of viewing pleasures promised by the film. However, what tends to be taken for granted, or dismissed as a simple contradiction, are the various ways in which *Falling Down* frustrates or fails to meet these expectations as its narrative unfolds. *Death Wish, Network,* and *Taxi Driver* are all in some respects linear narratives of an individual's descent into violence. Part of what made *Death Wish* controversial was its framing of this trajectory as a process of self-actualisation. Middle-class architect Paul Kersey (Charles Bronson) responds to the murder and rape of his wife and daughter by transforming from a social liberal who had been a conscientious objector to the Korean War, into an armed vigilante who pursues criminals and eliminates them in an increasingly elaborate and violent manner. The same narrative is repeated in each of the four sequels, with minor variations: Kersey begins each film living a privileged middle-class life before something, usually the victimisation of his loved ones, provokes him to resume his career as a vigilante. Moreover, he evades capture and punishment for his crimes, even – provocatively enough – attaining the approval of the police, tacit in *Death Wish*, explicit in *Death Wish 3* (1985). This linear narrative trajectory is conspicuously absent from *Falling Down*. More often than not, D-Fens's venting of his anger is generally associated with *his* 'falling down', and ultimately his being brought under the authority of the police, even if it might afford certain kinds of viewing pleasure to audiences. He is presented at his most negative in the early scene in Mr Lee's store, and at his most positive in the last 20 minutes of the film, when, alongside his increasing violence, he expresses tenderness to young children, stands up against wealth and privilege in the persons of the two golfers, and effectively commits suicide for his daughter's sake. Critics noticed these contradictions, but tended to dismiss them as either examples of the film's crudity or its evasion of responsibility. This left unconsidered how D-Fens's ambivalent status as hero *and* villain differs from the model established in the *Death Wish* series. In particular, the film's emphasis on his role as a father, dysfunctional as it is, and the character's strong yearning for domesticity and to 'go home', sets him apart from the lone male vigilante archetype, and links him to more exceptional cinematic precursors such as Neddy Merrill, the character played by Burt Lancaster in *The Swimmer* (1968).[6] Similarly, the film's emphasis on D-Fens's positive dealings with the African American protester and youths markedly distinguish him from the racially charged circumstances of the Bernhard Goetz case.

The notion that *Falling Down* represented a knowing revision of the 1970s vigilante movie was propounded in Julie Salamon's review in the *Wall Street Journal*. 'The filmmakers aren't out to make a crisp action fantasy' she argued. Rather, the 'disaffected man has no specific enemy or at least not one that he acknowledges; modern life is his enemy … He's an existential vigilante' (1993, p. A12). What is particularly telling about Salamon's reading is that she tries to understand the film's ambiguity (or lack of 'crispness') as itself being meaningful, rather than dismissing it or attributing it to the cynicism of the film-makers. There were similarities between this approach and that of prominent critics such as Richard Corliss (in *Time*) and Hal Hinson in the article already cited, who pondered the discontinuity between what they saw as *Falling Down*'s fundamental incoherence and formal failings as a movie, and its ability, in what was becoming a frequently used phrase, to strike a nerve. Though both had major reservations about the film's racial politics, Corliss wrote that the film had a value in having brought 'our uglier imaginings into focus' (1993, p. 63); while Hinson allowed that 'a film doesn't have to be great – or even very good – to be found important as a kind of cultural landmark' (1993).

Falling Down's pretensions as a social document were treated less sympathetically elsewhere, however. For some, Schumacher's and Douglas's claims to social and political significance acted as a smokescreen to legitimise pandering to violent revenge fantasies. This was Kenneth Turan's point when he called the film 'Charles Bronson's *Death Wish* with a bogus social conscience' (1993, p. 1), whilst David Ansen argued that the film, though frequently 'dumb', had 'pretensions [that] render it pernicious' (1993, p. 80). What was at stake here was the film's apparent sympathy with white middle-class rage and its orientation towards a paranoid racial politics, and this would come shortly to dominate controversy over the film.[7]

Negative Images: 'Race'

People associated with the objects of D-Fens's rage – especially the Korean shopkeeper and Latino gang members who are defined generically in the film by their 'race' or ethnicity – may well have found the film provocative under any circumstances. In the wake of the attacks on Korean-run businesses that had been such a prominent aspect of the 1992 disturbances, the portrayal of a Korean shopkeeper as D-Fens's first victim was viewed as particularly dangerous. Community advocacy groups such as the Media Action Network for Asian Americans, the Korean American Coalition, Women's Organization Reaching Koreans, and the newly formed Korean American Advocates for Justice, organised a range of responses. Various screenings were picketed, while in early March several groups met officially with Warner Bros representatives, including Joel Schumacher (Rauzi, 1993; Salisbury, 1993, p. 78). In an article in the *Los Angeles Times*, 22 March, Jeana H. Park, executive director of the Korean American Advocates for Justice, outlined a detailed critique of the scene in which D-Fens smashes up Mr Lee's store. Fiercely critical of Warner Bros, Schumacher, Smith, and Douglas, Jeana Park describes herself as being 'tired of seeing Korean Americans and other Asian Americans being enveloped in such a negative image that we are hated/labelled/rejected before we are known or understood'. This was to invoke the critique of 'negative images' that organisations such as the NAACP (National Association for Colored People) had been engaging in for decades. Most obviously, such critiques articulate a sense of defamation and outrage at the circulation of negative images; more subtly, they seek to contest the generic logic of ethnic stereotyping, whether in specific cultural texts such as films or in wider social representations. It is in this context that Park calls for more rounded, complex representations of Asian Americans, not in order to sanitise their image but to contest the dehumanising reduction of individuals to their presumed racial identity.[8]

    Falling Down's depiction of the Korean shopkeeper was by far the most prominent of its provocations against what was already being called 'political correctness', but it was by no means the only one. Critics routinely mentioned its stereotyping of Latino gang members, while it was also widely reported that the film had been protested by the National Center for Career Change, an organisation representing workers from the defence industry who had lost their jobs due to cuts in spending after the end of the Cold War. 'We issued a laid-off workers' survival guide', Bill Souveroff, a spokesperson for the Center, was quoted as saying, 'and street fighting is not one of the tips'. Symptomatically, Souveroff expressed concerns at negative stereotyping, worrying that Douglas's 'cartoonish flattop and pocket pen protector' would 'stigmatize all defence workers' (Appelo, 1993).

Negative Images: The City of Los Angeles

'You want to see sick?' D-Fens asks Beth when she suggests that he needs treatment for mental illness, 'Take a walk around this town. That's sick'. In the wake of the riots/uprising, the public image of Los Angeles was a sensitive topic, and its depiction in *Falling Down* was received as a kind of provocation. Several critics noted that the film was reviewed significantly less positively in the city than elsewhere in the United States, while from New York it was observed that the city was 'in uproar' over the movie (Douglas, 1993; Reinhold, 1993). That may have been an exaggeration, but aside from the protests against the negative stereotyping of Asian Americans, the next most prominent bone of contention was the film's portrayal of the city itself as a balkanised, territorialised place fractured along lines of ethnicity, class, and gender.

A few days before *Falling Down* was released, Jack Mathews (1993) kicked off consideration of the issue in a *Los Angeles Times* article headed 'La-La Land No More'. He linked the film not to the thriller genre, as in most of the opening weekend reviews, but to the succession of films in which Los Angeles had played 'the city of diversity – and division': *Colors* (1988), *Grand Canyon* (1991), *Boyz N the Hood* (1991), and 'half a dozen other gritty L.A. movies coming this year'. Mathews even-handedly set out the two extremes that would come to circumscribe debates over *Falling Down*:

> There are scenes in some of these movies, those made by white
> directors, that play off racial stereotypes and into the urban paranoia
> of the new white minority. At the same time, those scenes do reflect
> the confusion, fear and frustration felt by people who, in less than
> two decades, have seen their hometown turn into something foreign
> to them.

The sense of *Falling Down* as portraying problems that were specific to
the racial geography of Los Angeles was taken up elsewhere (Reeves,
1993; Reinhold, 1993). Meanwhile, as the film proved popular across the
United States, taking $8 million on its first weekend and topping the box
office for three weeks, the *Los Angeles Times* reported protests and violent
incidents similar to those depicted in the film. The *Times* would give over
many column inches to discussion of the film during the next month,
much of which emphasised the significance of its location. At one level,
the newspaper seems to have taken it as an offence to civic pride. After
Turan's highly critical review described earlier, on 7 March it published a
short piece by Peter H. King (1993), who more or less retraced the steps
of D-Fens from downtown to Venice Beach. Emerging unscathed, King
questioned the accuracy of the film's depiction of L.A., concluding that 'it
is still a pretty good place to live'. A week or so later, political columnist
Bob Baker (1993) complained that 'Last spring's riots created a wave of
Hollywood interest in exploiting Los Angeles as a pressure-cooker of
horrors'. Baker's sociological and political critique was part of a three-page
broadside unleashed on the film in the *Times*'s 'Calendar' section on 15
March. In 'Are WE Falling Apart?', Robin Rauzi gathered the views of
Los Angelenos who had seen the film. In short the answer was 'no'. Whilst
acknowledging certain tensions, the article tells a story of ethnic harmony
which was distinctly at odds with the film. Meanwhile Peter Rainer (1993)
argued that *Falling Down* 'isn't some all-purpose cry of disgust. It's the howl
of a scared, white, urban middle-class man'. The serious critiques launched
by Rainer and Baker expanded the genre focus seen in the early reviews by

reference to a heightened sense of the film's resonance with local, regional, and national controversies. Both cite the film's thriller precursors – Rainer calls it a 'smorgasbord *Death Wish*' – but both are more interested in its wider political implications. Both make it clear that there was much more at stake than mere civic pride.

In Baker's view (1993), *Falling Down* is spectacularly hypocritical in its relation to city politics, blaming immigrants and the poor for the urban blight which had been caused by middle-class voters, like D-Fens and his neighbours, turning their backs on the inner city and thus depriving it of the tax revenues necessary to provide public services and schools. He imagines D-Fens, or Bill Foster, learning the true reasons for the lack of civility he encounters:

> Let Bill discover how his fellow citizens voted down tax measures to build rapid transit, keeping his freeways clogged, and kept voting for Reagan-esque politicians who sold government as society's enemy … Let Bill discover how the Bradley Administration, obsessed with making Los Angeles a safe place for downtown development, ducked Los Angeles' gang crisis during the 1980s until it was too late. Let him discover how the political Establishment avoided coming to grips with the social costs of immigration.

This point was echoed by L.A. Deputy Mayor Mark Fabiani, who was reported as saying that the Douglas character was probably a Reaganite who had voted to cut taxes and public services (quoted in Reinhold, 1993). Peter Rainer's article (1993) also related the film to party politics, but in the realm of culture rather than economics. For him, *Falling Down* was a 'last-minute whammy from the Reagan–Bush era that finally makes explicit the social divisiveness that was implicit in so many of the films from that period'.

The *Los Angeles Times* printed another, more balanced, set of responses to the film a week later (Douglas, 1993; D'Addiero, 1993; Park, 1993), but already the debate over its 'social divisiveness' was spiralling out of the immediate context of Southern California. The specifics of the film's location had taken on diagnostic and symptomatic significance in relation to wider debates in the United States. If this 'new mythical L.A.' had supplanted the 'old mythical L.A. of endless summers' (King, 1993) the implications were national as well as regional. On the one hand, from socially liberal and leftist perspectives, the city provided a kind of test case of the effects of Reaganite Republicans' national policies of cutting taxes and government spending. On the other hand, from a right-wing perspective, the breakdown of aspects of civil society in *Falling Down*'s Los Angeles could be attributed to large-scale immigration and policies of multiculturalism. Either way, specific concerns about the film's accurate or exaggerated representation of conditions in Los Angeles were giving way to its wider construction as a 'zeitgeist' movie.

Newsweek

The politicised debate over *Falling Down* attained national significance in the last week of March 1993, when D-Fens could be seen staring out through his broken glasses from the cover of *Newsweek* magazine. The 4,000 word cover story by David Gates, entitled 'White Male Paranoia: Are They the New Victims or Just Bad Sports?' used the film as a starting point to examine the latest twist in American identity politics. *Falling Down*, according to Gates (1993), argued that 'the fashionable revisionist reading of American history and culture that makes the white male the bad guy has triumphed...and it's made him not just defensive, but paranoid'. Quoting businesswomen, legislators, sociologists, psychiatrists, members of the men's movement, Christian leaders, firefighters, and judges, as well as economic data and opinion polls especially commissioned from Gallup, the article went on to examine 'the beleaguered white male in multicultural America'.

Gates's *Newsweek* article concerned itself with a basic paradox: how was it, when white males continued to dominate everything from the Forbes 400 (people worth more than $265 million), Congress, state governorships, and tenured college faculty, to daily newspaper editorships and television news, that so many white men were thinking of themselves as underdogs and victims, as manifested in the popularity of figures such as 'shock jock' Howard Stern and political commentator Rush Limbaugh, and the growth of conservative strains of the men's movement? A likely answer might have been sought in the changing labour patterns of the post-industrial economy, where traditionally male-orientated manufacturing jobs were in steep decline and the expanding service-led economy favoured 'feminine' qualities. However, interestingly enough, the article neither examined such economic data nor did much to distinguish between white men of different socio-economic classes. Rather, it positioned economic factors as exacerbating a dynamic that is essentially cultural and political. 'White male paranoia', the piece argued at its core,

> isn't old-fashioned white liberal guilt, it's atavistic racial and sexual dread, and it achieves critical mass when a rapidly contracting economy becomes overcrowded. White men used to feel guilty about what they had or what they'd done. Now they're required to feel guilty about what they are.

This view crystallises an argument of sociologist Michael Kimmel, whom Gates quoted explicitly. One of the most prominent academic writers on masculinity, Kimmel was associated with the liberal wing of the men's movement, and has served as spokesperson for the National Organisation of Men Against Sexism. In his seminal *Manhood in America: A Cultural History* (1995), now in its third edition, Kimmel outlines his position, which can be summarised as acknowledging the pain and confusion felt by men as dominant forms of masculinity come under criticism, and seeking more 'democratic' forms of gender identity in dialogue with feminism. Gates's article, however, downplayed the attempts at progressive intervention that Kimmel and others were making, while reiterating their emphasis on the *cultural* rather than economic causes of the crisis.

In *Newsweek*, then, white male paranoia was explained by cultural and political factors: the prevalence of depictions of white men as weak or ridiculous figures on television, the effects of affirmative action programmes, and newly elected President Bill Clinton's widely reported determination to appoint a cabinet that 'looks like America'. In retrospect, what is quite surprising about the article, in a mainstream publication, is the lack of sympathy it demonstrates towards those white men who experience cultural marginalisation. 'White male paranoia' is presented as a response to real cultural and political factors, not a form of false consciousness; it is understandable but, as the defence of a privilege that is slipping away, illegitimate. 'White male paranoia' functions in the article as a political given, which can only be accepted or disavowed. The piece imagines the sense of grievance as always already politicised in gendered and racial terms, precluding any resolution either by reference to class and economics, or to feminism in the manner propounded by Kimmel. Instead, it presents a struggle for power in American society as a zero-sum game, where for some to make gains, others must lose. Although *Falling Down* serves as little more than the pretext for the article, dropping out of sight after the first couple of paragraphs, this sense of the intractability of political differences might well be seen to be reproduced in the narrative of D-Fens.

The most sympathetic depictions of white men in Gates's article are of firefighters who believe that they have been passed over due to affirmative action programmes for women and African Americans. One of them is quoted as complaining that 'If you're black and belong to a black group you're an activist. If you're white and you belong to a white group, you're an asshole. Nobody supports the KKK – I don't. But there's nothing for a white guy to join'. Highlighting the plight of such men, the article implies that their understanding of their own situation is flawed, but fails to offer one that is more progressive or helpful. It is these men who seem the closest real-life counterparts to D-Fens, who does not himself fit the article's definition of 'white male paranoia' very well, as his abiding emotion seems to be frustration at not being able to perform his role as a father, rather than resentment at a supposed requirement to feel guilty. Significantly enough, although Prendergast is not mentioned throughout the piece, he seems to fit that description perfectly, and to emancipate himself from it in the climactic sequence of the film.

Crossfire

On 29 March, while the Oscar ceremony was unfolding, the news channel CNN devoted its *Crossfire* talk show to *Falling Down*. Running from 1982 until 2005, the show's format pitted against each other two co-hosts defined as being from the political left and right, each of whom select guests to discuss topical issues from contesting perspectives. *Crossfire* has been highly influential, instrumental in the fusion of news, politics, and entertainment that is now common on the major US television networks and a staple of Fox News and MSNBC, and in promoting the 'punditocracy' of figures who blur the boundaries between journalism, political comment, and office-holders (Barkin, 2003, pp. 77–78). At this time, columnist and *New Republic* editor Michael Kinsley was the left liberal host of the programme. The position of right-wing host alternated between Patrick Buchanan, who had been a speechwriter and advisor in Richard Nixon's administration, and had stood the previous year in the Republican primaries against incumbent President George W. Bush, and John Sununu, recently Chief of Staff in Bush's White House. Though the topic was one close to Buchanan's political interests, it was Sununu's turn to act as the host on the right, eliciting the support of Barry Slotnick, who had been the defending attorney for the 'subway vigilante' Bernhard Goetz at his 1986–1987 trial. Kinsley meanwhile had Michael Kimmel, the academic sociologist quoted in Gates's *Newsweek* article, as his guest on the left.

    Crossfire itself has come under fire from various perspectives. Noam Chomsky objected that a wide spectrum of dissent was either sidelined or co-opted by the show's reduction of issues to a mere two sides. Its cancellation in January 2005 is widely attributed to criticisms voiced several months earlier on the show by the political satirist Jon Stewart, to the effect that it subjugated detailed and in-depth examination of issues to entertainment values. As an example of what might be called 'controversy culture', the transformation of political debate into television drama, the show was itself in some ways a counterpart to *Falling Down*'s status as a movie that deliberately courted controversy. On the night, perhaps predictably given the *Crossfire* format, no clear winner of the argument emerged. Slotnick's attempts to persuade the studio audience that D-Fens stood for the feelings of decent honest people were met with ironic laughter. Yet Kimmel was scarcely more successful when he tried to explain the existence of a crisis of masculinity in culture, while at the same time trying to expose its lack of an economic base. However, in one respect at least, the show did cement a political position. Despite its even-handed format, on this occasion even Kimmel and Kinsley tended to accept the conservative view of identity politics that emphasised its dependence on discourses of victimhood. As with Gates's use of Kimmel's work in *Newsweek*, the framing of a 'crisis of white masculinity' in the popular media precluded the liberating traditions of identity politics.

Defences and Counter-Arguments

Several of the key players in the production of *Falling Down*, especially Joel Schumacher and Michael Douglas, publicly responded to the criticisms of the film that followed its release. Both disputed the early readings of the film as a distorted portrayal of Los Angeles, emphasising that it was intended as a microcosm of American society. Schumacher took the unusual step of meeting personally with some of the Korean American groups. He adopted a conciliatory, if possibly rather patronising, position, explaining that the scenes that they regarded as offensive had been written and shot before the riots (cited in Salisbury, 1993, p. 78). Michael Douglas was reportedly less apologetic and more provocative, a difference of perspective detectable in the contributions of star and director to the commentary track on the 2009 Blu-ray release. He insisted on the right to portray a character who was in part racist, and observed that 'You cannot make a movie today if you have to worry whether you're politically correct' (Parker, 2011, p. 334). Douglas also shrugged off responsibility for exacerbating any 'image problem' that Koreans may have had (Parker, 2011, p. 335). His most frequent concern was about audiences' failure to appreciate the complexity of his performance, and in particular the polarisation of views into pro- and anti-D-Fens positions (Salisbury, 1993, p. 78; Douglas, 2009). In the 2009 Blu-ray commentary, Douglas bemoans the lack of sophistication of viewers who regard D-Fens as a hero, maintaining that the character he plays is, as he puts it, 'nuts' from the beginning (Schumacher, 1993/2009). This was an argument made plangently by Kirk Douglas, who had insisted, in the wake of the early critical reviews, that D-Fens was the villain of the movie, and expressed pride that his son 'had the guts to play a prejudiced, middle-class nerd' (Douglas, 1993).

More generally, Schumacher and Michael Douglas defended the film as 'healthy', either making visible a neglected set of people, or drawing attention to a social problem, or allowing viewers to purge their frustrations and resentments. As Schumacher put it in one interview: 'When you strike a nerve, people will scream. And they scream *loud*' (quoted in Salisbury 1993, p. 76). Both Schumacher and Douglas defined the social problem in question in specifically identity-driven terms, discussing D-Fens as the embodiment of white male anger that was identified in popular media by Gates, Rainer, and Baker, and on *Crossfire*. Schumacher set up the film specifically as a counterpart of recent African American films that had portrayed urban violence. 'As I saw it', Schumacher told an interviewer,

> this movie was reflecting attitudes in society. Usually, the movies that reflect anger in the street do so from the standpoint of Afro-Amer-

icans, a race thing. The fact is, they are not the only angry people in America. This is a multiracial, multicultural city, and the story could have been on any six o'clock news. I tried to give it a face and a soul. (quoted in Parker, 2011, p. 331)

These remarks suggest a complicated relationship with African American cinema. Schumacher could be read as acknowledging the achievements of film-makers such as Spike Lee and John Singleton in films such as *Do the Right Thing* (1989) and *Boyz N the Hood*, and attempting to emulate them. As such, he is reflecting significant changes to the American film industry effected by the emergence of African American directors in the late 1980s and early 1990s. But a less liberal interpretation is also possible, whereby Schumacher might be read as assuming that his predecessors' work was limited by its African American context, and that the definitive representation of anger in the street could be made only from the ostensibly broader perspective of racial whiteness.[9] Elsewhere, and in some contrast to Douglas's descriptions of the film, Schumacher emphasised the more quotidian and universal aspects of D-Fens's frustration, suggesting that 'his release is so identifiable to all our angers because they're simple ones... [g]etting out of a car in the middle of traffic; the desire to maybe pull out a gun if you don't get something your way'; albeit that his behaviour is 'abhorrent' (Simpson, 1993, p. 77). The distinction between D-Fens as everyman, and D-Fens as angry white male, is of course the crux of much of the controversy about the film.

These are credible positions, consistent on the one hand with Schumacher's professionalism and his previous engagement with African American culture as a writer on *Car Wash* (1976) and *The Wiz* (1978), and on the other with the reputation for provocation developed by Douglas from *One Flew over the Cuckoo's Nest*, through *The China Syndrome* and *Fatal Attraction* to *Basic Instinct*. In the last analysis, no doubt as much for artistic as commercial reasons, such positions disclaim any responsibility for a film's social or cultural influence, and invite viewers and critics to make what they can of the movie. Much popular film journalism and biography reiterates this logic, framing the topicality of Douglas's films within the immediate context of film production and consumption. As John Parker's biography *Michael Douglas: Acting on Instinct* demonstrates, writers in this area employ ideas of professional and artistic integrity in order to judge the provocative roles that Douglas played in the late 1980s and early 1990s. Parker celebrates *Fatal Attraction*, *Basic Instinct*, and subsequently *Disclosure*, for their topicality, while defending Douglas from being identified too closely with the character flaws, weaknesses, and sometimes racism and misogyny exhibited by the characters. Significantly, he validates Douglas's deliberate challenge to 'political correctness', which he glosses as the prescriptive or self-censoring requirement 'that movies today should in some way provide a formula for the conduct of society'. This underwrites a positive view of *Falling Down* as 'a presentation of facts, an accumulation of disturbing incidents that could happen, were happening, with no sub-text and no last-reel solution' (Parker, 2011, p. 334). The problem with this approach is that it sidelines key questions about the film. What exactly are the facts publicised by *Falling Down*? Presumably, that white men are angry. But what proportion of white males were angry? Are they more or less angry than other people? And did their anger have a legitimate cause? Were these causes economic, and if so were they the inevitable result of the reduction in arms production at the end of the Cold War, or were they due to the decline in manufacturing more or less deliberately overseen by Reaganite economic policy? Or were they social and cultural feelings of displacement and marginalisation in the face of perceived social and cultural gains by women and people of colour (gains which were clearly patchy at best). And more importantly perhaps, at whom was this anger directed? The beneficiaries of generations of struggle for equality – struggles which even now have not yielded a level playing field? Or political or institutional targets?

What is striking about *Falling Down* is that the film ticks all of these boxes. Three angry white men, D-Fens, Prendergast, and Nick, the neo-Nazi surplus store owner, between them target physically or verbally a Korean shopkeeper, Latino gang members, homeless people, burger bar staff, road construction workers, city government and its 'inflated budgets', wealthy golfers, D-Fens's ex-wife, Prendergast's wife, the police chief who is Prendergast's boss, two homosexual men, a Latina police officer, and one another. This could be interpreted as simply a random succession of targets, or, more credibly, it could be organised according to the positions and trajectories of the three angry white men. It could also be taken as a microcosm of a balkanised nation split into warring identity groups, having lost whatever communal sense of national identity that it once may have had. Yet running through this solidly identity-based framework is a thread of economics. In one of his final speeches, D-Fens describes himself as 'not economically viable', a phrase he has taken from an African American man protesting outside a bank. Though the phrase, tellingly, means different things – the protester believes the bank employed the term as an excuse to deny him a loan, the real reason being racial discrimination, while for D-Fens it is a simple matter of being unemployed and unable to provide economically for his child – it establishes a link between the two figures as potentially sharing a class position which belies their evident racial differences and their abilities to control and focus their anger. Conversely, where Prendergast's low status in the workplace and his imminent retirement might have put him symbolically in the 'not economically viable' camp throughout most of the film, his situation is reversed by his killing of D-Fens and he ends the film triumphantly insisting that 'I'm still a cop'.

One response to this state of affairs might be to adopt a 'postmodern' approach and simply accept as equally valid all the various interpretations and implications of *Falling Down*. The film is indeed a kind of focus for competing political and cultural views and for individual investments and fantasies. This book tries to render its openness to debate, while also seeking to determine the significance of *how* the film defined discussion, and especially the terms in which it courted controversy. Not only do these terms in many instances correspond to specific positions in American identity politics, but the film itself knowingly invokes cinematic forms – characterisations and narratives from the western, police procedural, and thriller genres – as a means of playing out and resolving white male anger.

The Question of Identification

The crucial point of discussion here has been the extent to which D-Fens is normalised and is the subject of audience identification. Several points are germane here. First, there are echoes of 1980s debates over home viewing of films in the concerns over D-Fens attracting audience identification with violent attacks on the Korean shopkeeper and his shooting of the gang member in cold blood. To such objections, the notion that audiences are progressively alienated from D-Fens is immaterial, as the problem with the film from this perspective is that it offers an irresponsible and potentially dangerous viewing pleasure, a bad lesson that could be imitated in real-life. However, more interesting debates have focused on the complicated and non-linear ways in which the film represents violence and identity, ways in which production design (which portrays Los Angeles as a forest of confusing and hostile signs, many of them in Spanish), editing, performance, and narrative, alternatively universalise and particularise D-Fens, drawing audiences in, then alienating them, only to draw them in again to his perspective. This also serves to differentiate it from thrillers, which superficially resemble *Falling Down* but which tend to pivot on a single traumatic moment, such as the killing of the wife of architect Paul Kersey (Charles Bronson) and the rape of his daughter in *Death Wish,* or from westerns, such as, classically, *The Searchers* that narrate a linear descent into violence or estrangement from civilised behaviour. *Falling Down*, though sometimes represented in these terms, does not actually follow this pattern. To take one example, in the climactic scene on Venice pier, D-Fens looks

at his most deranged (see Figure 10 in Part 4), and Prendergast accuses him of intending to kill Beth and Adele. To be sure, D-Fens's aggression towards Beth is potentially terrifying, but the entire film goes out of its way to emphasise his kindness to and gentleness with children, and this scene is no different, emphasising that D-Fens puts down his gun twice to talk to Adele, and, as has already been noted, ultimately sacrifices himself for her economic welfare. As critic John Gabriel concluded after interviewing British viewers of the film, in one of the few pieces of systematic audience research on *Falling Down*, the film elicited 'episodic and transitory forms of identification and recognition' (1996, p. 150). The common denominator among the large range of views of D-Fens, Gabriel found, was that of having mixed reactions.

In support of his ambivalence about D-Fens, Schumacher also tells a story about one viewer's mixed reactions to the film. In a 1993 interview and in his contribution to the commentary track of the 2009 edition of *Falling Down*, he quotes Annette Bening, who but for taking a career break to have a baby may well have starred opposite Douglas in *Basic Instinct*, and would go on to play opposite him in *The American President* (1995). When she walked out of seeing the film in New York, according to Schumacher, 'it was daylight and at first she felt, "What kind of world am I bringing my baby up in?" Then as she got further down the block she thought, "Any one of these people could be Michael's character". And by the time she reached the kerb she thought, "*I* could be that person"' (cited in Salisbury, p. 77).[10] The way that Bening's reactions to the film were conditioned by her own lived experience of New York corroborates the notion that the urban experience depicted in *Falling Down* is a general condition, in North American cities at least. The anecdote obviously testifies to the intense audience identification that D-Fens inspired in many viewers. But Bening's reported reactions also suggest an aspect of the experience of viewing the film that tended to escape the polemics of those who weighed into the first round of the *Falling Down* controversy: that audiences made multiple and *shifting* identifications with the film's protagonists.

The question of identification in *Falling Down* is a multifaceted one. At one level, the film focalises anger over the perceived breakdown of civil society. Yet it also deliberately, and frequently, represents D-Fens's anger as fundamentally mis-directed. Aggressive and seedy as Michael Paul Chan's Korean shopkeeper is, inflation and the economics of small-scale retail in downtown Los Angeles are more likely to be responsible for his prices than is naked profiteering. Similarly, many viewers and critics regarded D-Fens as holding the homeless people, Whammyburger personnel, and construction workers responsible for economic conditions and corporate and municipal policies over which they have no control. For many, this maps on to a fundamentally 'paranoid' position, in which the cultural, social, and economic gains of people of colour and women since the 1960s are seen both as victimising white males and betraying egalitarian American traditions. Criticisms of *Falling Down* as an articulation of white male paranoia tended to emphasise the ways in which the film enlists audience identification with D-Fens and Prendergast on the basis of their victimisation as white males, and to miss – or to dismiss as a manipulative ruse – elements of the film that position them as more universal figures whose frustrations transcend gendered and racial identity, and other elements that alienate viewers from D-Fens. Such aspects complicate the controversy provoked by *Falling Down*'s dramatisation of the anger felt by a specific identity group, namely economically disenfranchised white men, who had previously enjoyed the privileged status of belonging to the mainstream of American society.

In order to fully explore these questions of identification, it is necessary to understand the debates over identity that were taking place in the United States in the early 1990s, and to bring to bear on *Falling Down* the ideas about film and identity developed since the 1970s in academic film theory. The next part of this book will do just that, putting *Falling Down* into the wider historical context of the battles over American identity known as the 'culture wars', and showing how *Falling Down* and other movies of the time led critics to rethink several of the key elements of academic film theory. Part 4 then goes on to apply these insights in an analysis of a number of the film's key scenes.

✖ PART 3

THE 'CRISIS OF WHITE MASCULINITY'

An Ambiguous Film

What makes *Falling Down* truly controversial, as opposed to simply causing offence or gaining notoriety, is its combination of provocation, ambiguity, and incoherence. If protests and pickets demonstrated that it had struck a nerve, the debates that unfolded in newspapers, magazines, and on television demonstrated the film's imbrication in the so-called culture wars, the backlash against the identity politics movements on behalf of African American Civil Rights, feminism, and gay liberation. As we have seen, the film was widely discussed both for its use of what were seen as negative stereotypes of ethnicity, and its address to the phenomenon of white male anger. However, no consensus emerged about its precise orientation. Janus-like, *Falling Down*'s evocation of a balkanised Los Angeles suggested the nightmare vision of multiculturalism conjured up by the political right, yet also depicted the consequences of infrastructural neglect that resulted from right-wing policies of cutting taxes and municipal budgets. The film's protagonist – or antagonist – was simultaneously marked as one of the angry white males frustrated at his loss of privilege and presented as an everyman figure standing up against a society that has lost the values of civility, respect, and community. Thus D-Fens exemplifies widely shared frustrations at modern urban life, a pervasive sense of the betrayal of the liberating potential central to the self-image of the United States, *and* special pleading on behalf of what was and remains one of the most privileged identity groups in the country. The film's advertising tagline, reproduced on movie posters and video/DVD packaging from 1993 until 2009, asks viewers to see him as 'An ordinary man at war with the everyday world', one who not only commands a certain amount of audience sympathy but who in important ways also embodies a common condition of the American 1990s. Made redundant by post-Cold-War downsizing, D-Fens in his own estimation 'did everything they asked me to', but loses job, status, family, and eventually, his life. Yet the film deliberately particularises this story in racial and gendered terms. D-Fens's hostility towards his ex-wife, and his aggression when provoked by characters such as Mr Lee, the Korean shopkeeper, and members of the Latino gang, seem to cater to a very specifically white and reactionary form of nostalgia. His explicit desires to 'go home' and his demand to roll back prices to 1965 may elicit sympathy from a range of viewers, but they define what is wrong with America from a particular gendered and racial perspective: through a nostalgia for a moment before new immigrants changed the country's identity, before second-wave feminists challenged patriarchal power, and before the national character was stained by the war in Vietnam. It was of course these latter elements that earned D-Fens the 'white male paranoia' tag and led to the film's being regarded by so many critics as part of a backlash against the identity politics movements, as a superheated throwback to the Reagan–Bush years, or as tapping into the dissatisfaction with mainstream politics that in 1992 sustained the campaign of third-party Presidential candidate Ross Perot.

The question of D-Fens's ambivalence was intensified by the 1992 riots/uprising. On the one hand, he could be seen as the everyman figure, a focal point for the anger felt by the frustrated, the disenfranchised, and the marginalised. Yet, on the other hand, D-Fens's own racial and gendered identity were crucial elements in forging his anger. Either way, what heated the argument was the film's apparent commitment to both sides at once, as a liberal indictment of social order, and as voicing a paranoid wish to return to a fantasy America where the power of white men was unquestioned, and immigrant populations from Asia and South and Central America were either non-existent or invisible. As in the case of *Basic Instinct* a year earlier, a Michael Douglas picture had stepped into politicised debates over identity. However, the context in which those debates were taking place had shifted decisively. The protests against *Basic Instinct* initiated by GLAAD, the Gay and Lesbian Alliance Against Defamation, operated along the lines of positive/negative images, stereotyping, normalisation, and marginalisation that had been pioneered decades earlier in the field of racial representation by organisations such as the NAACP, and taken up by second-wave feminists and the gay liberation movement in the

1970s (see Simkin, 2013). Such debates generally concerned themselves with the depiction of people of colour, women, and homosexuals and their marginalisation. The *Falling Down* controversy, as we have just seen, began in these terms, with attention focused on the stereotypical depiction of the Korean shopkeeper and Latino gang members, but quickly settled on the figure of D-Fens and his ambiguous status. As Schumacher's and Douglas's comments suggest, they could never quite decide whether D-Fens was an everyman, or represented white males as a special case. The cultural, political, and academic contexts of the early 1990s made this ambiguity particularly meaningful.

Falling Down epitomised the 1990s twist in identity politics that is summed up by the phrase the 'crisis of white masculinity'. This is a potentially confusing term precisely because it has been used in a variety of contexts. It embraces the notion of 'white male paranoia' described in Gates's *Newsweek* article, and the 'angry white males' who emerged as a political constituency around the presidential candidacies of Patrick Buchanan and Ross Perot in 1992, and who were seen as the major force behind the Republican landslide in the mid-term elections of 1994 that gave large majorities to the Republicans in both houses of Congress, under the leadership of Newt Gingrich. As an unemployed white male who seems to resent his ex-wife and non-whites, D-Fens might be regarded as a typical 'angry white male'. But the 'crisis of white masculinity' suggests something related, but different: neither reaction to a perceived loss of group status, nor directly a political or social crisis, but a *crisis of representation*. Put simply, the phrase suggests the calling into question of the ways that white masculinity as an identity formation had asserted its dominance by embodying the norm, the unmarked, the universal. For decades if not centuries, by a kind of cultural sleight of hand, whiteness and masculinity signalled both specific, exclusive racial and gendered identities, while also occupying the place of the unmarked and the universal. In gender terms, this blurring is most obvious in the use of words such as 'man' and 'mankind' as ostensibly non-gendered and commonly human categories. The racial counterpart of such language

is seen for example in news items which specify racial identity only for
non-whites, a practice which has decreased markedly since the 1980s. In
the late 1980s and early 1990s, under pressure from criticism mobilised by
previously marginalised groups, and from their innovative representations
of identity which were increasingly refracted in mainstream American
culture, the traditional power-bearing forms of white masculinity were
thrown into relief and remade. More than any other Hollywood movie,
Falling Down exemplifies this pivotal moment. In order to understand the
film fully, therefore, it is necessary to outline the 'crisis of white masculinity'
historically and to consider how it was addressed in Hollywood film before
Falling Down, and to review its impact on critical approaches to 'race' and
gender.

The Culture Wars

The 'culture wars' or 'cultural war' is in itself not a construction of the
identity movements, but of the right-wing backlash against them, which saw
and continues to see multiculturalism as a threat to traditional American,
or western, values. The notion was elaborated by Patrick Buchanan, former
aide and advisor to Richard Nixon, who in 1992 ran as a candidate for the
Republican Party nomination for the Presidency on an overtly ideological,
'values-led' platform. While *Falling Down* was in post-production, in
August 1992, Buchanan delivered what has become known as the 'culture
wars speech' to the Republican Party Convention in Houston. At its climax,
Buchanan stated:

> My friends, this election is about much more than who gets what. It is
> about who we are. It is about what we believe. It is about what we stand
> for as Americans. There is a religious war going on in our country for
> the soul of America. It is a cultural war, as critical to the kind of nation
> we will one day be as was the Cold War itself. (1992a; 1992b)

The key ideological move here, fairly transparently, is to equate the challenge to the idea of white male power, as exemplified by, say, the address of Bill Clinton's presidential campaign to women and non-whites, with a challenge to the best American traditions. What threatened to corrupt America's soul, according to Buchanan, was the support for abortion, equal rights for homosexuals, and the inclusion of women in combat units – which he termed 'radical feminism' but which were quite simply the obvious results of the liberation struggles of women and gay men and lesbians. What is worth noting is that, at this time, Buchanan represented a much more overtly ideological view of social policy than did the mainstream of the Republican Party, which was represented by George W. Bush, who had decisively defeated Buchanan's challenge in the primaries. The Convention speech was framed as bringing the 'Buchanan brigades', the 3 million who had voted for Buchanan in the primaries, on board Bush's much less ideological campaign.

Buchanan remains a vocal critic of affirmative action programmes and a political figurehead for angry white males. It may well have been a perceived association with his rhetoric that generated some of the more vitriolic comments in the newspaper reviews of *Falling Down*. What is particularly suggestive is Peter Rainer's notion that the film made explicit a socially divisive agenda that had remained implicit in films of the Reagan–Bush era due to their lack of appetite for controversy (1993; discussed in Part 2 earlier); something that might well be regarded as a parallel to the emergence of Buchanan's overtly ideological stance compared with what was then the mainstream of the Republican Party. As more than one critic implied, the film perhaps traded on the affective power of D-Fens's extreme reactions, even as the film-makers disavowed him (Willis, 1997, p. 19).

Was there an Economic Basis to the 'Crisis of White Masculinity'?

A range of cultural, social, and political developments in the early 1990s, from Homer Simpson and other stereotypes on television, to Bill Clinton's determination to choose a cabinet that would 'look like America', may have undermined the status of white masculinity. Even the election of another white male as president in November 1992 represented a sort of political defeat for white men in general, only 37 per cent of whom voted for Clinton – 40 per cent voted for George W. Bush, and 20 per cent for Ross Perot. But one of the most compelling arguments made by Buchanan was an economic one, namely that under pressure from economic changes and affirmative action programmes, white men were losing their jobs and finding it harder to remain in high-paying, white-collar, and professional employment. This was potentially reflected in *Falling Down,* despite the narrative explanation that D-Fens was rendered surplus to requirements by the peace dividend. (Douglas's next movie, *Disclosure*, would rehearse several stories of a white male being displaced unfairly by a female worker.)

It was precisely the manufacturing jobs, now in decline, that had provided post-war generations of white men with what David Roediger (1999) terms the 'wages of whiteness'. But were middle-class white men like Bill Foster especially hard hit economically in the early 1990s? In racial terms, the answer is no. A detailed study using data from the Panel Study of Income Dynamics by sociologists Debra Branch McBrier and George Wilson specifically investigated the effect of 'race' on the incidence and process of downward occupational mobility for white-collar workers during the 1990s. They concluded that:

> [R]elative to White workers, African Americans suffered a higher incidence of downward occupational mobility, especially to blue-collar destinations, and the process by which African Americans fell down the occupational queue was less strongly predicted by traditional causal factors such as supply-side characteristics and job–labour market characteristics. (2004, p. 283)

Whites were hit no harder than non-whites by the changes in the labour market in the late 1980s and 1990s; in fact, African Americans suffered the most. Just when, as McBrier and Wilson put it, African Americans 'were poised to make their biggest upwardly mobile strides…the white-collar economy began to transition…[and] opportunities for upward structural mobility began to wane' (2004, p. 284). Nevertheless McBrier and Wilson do note several economic and social trends that are relevant to D-Fens's status as an 'ordinary man' who has become 'not economically viable'. After the depression of the late 1980s and early 1990s, McBrier and Wilson argue, corporate labour policies shifted dramatically away from long-term employment contracts and internal labour market protections towards downsizing, even in periods of growth, thus reducing the core workforce, especially mid-level management and professional ranks (2004, p. 284). This 'lean and mean' corporate style hit white-collar workers disproportionately hard: 'Whereas only one third of all displaced workers in the early 1980s had last held a white-collar job, by the 1990s [in fact, before 1995] more than one half of all displaced workers were formerly white-collar job occupants' (2004, p. 286).

The pace of the changes noted by McBrier and Wilson has accelerated faster since 1993. How might D-Fens's story refract these significant and far-reaching changes in the economic status of the American middle-class? As his white shirt and pocket pen-protector (over)emphasise, D-Fens had been a white-collar worker. He might have become an icon for what is at the time of writing called the 'squeezed middle' – so why did he not do so? The answer lies partly in the character's fundamental lack of understanding of his own situation, and partly in the film's lack of interest in exploring the corporate changes that, to be fair, have become much clearer in retrospect. Rather than being portrayed as a victim of corporate policy, D-Fens is represented with all the pathos that goes with economic, social, and cultural obsolescence. The drawing instruments that Prendergast finds in his room identify him as a practitioner of a specialist skill that is no longer required; he is not only a missile builder in a post-Cold-War age, he is an analogue worker in a world going digital.

In the highly influential *Stiffed: The Betrayal of the Modern Man* (1999) Susan Faludi traces back the cultural and social decline of male power in the 1990s to the 'closing of the American job' (Faludi, 1999, pp. 51–102): the decline in American manufacturing jobs which went hand in hand with the cultural ideals of authoritative, 'hard-body' masculinity. It is important to differentiate between differently racialised masculinities to a greater extent than is done in *Stiffed*; nevertheless Faludi's work offers an important conceptual innovation in thinking through the relationships between economic, and social and cultural 'crises' of masculinity. Perhaps the most important insight in *Stiffed* is that what had been the mutually reinforcing economic and cultural construction of 'manhood' as American masculinity was defined during the Cold War, had become a double bind for American men. Not only were they finding it harder to get and to stay in work, but their very understanding of masculinity as independent and confrontational sabotaged their ability to adapt to the changing labour market, or to adopt the communal responses used to some effect at least by the identity politics movements.

D-Fens could be regarded as an archetype of the men described by Faludi as being 'stiffed' in both of these ways. First, in having 'done everything they told me to', he exemplifies the condition of having worked hard at the normative forms of masculinity, only to find that instead of obtaining the expected economic and social rewards, he is cast aside from the workplace and excluded from the home. Second, his wondering 'I'm the bad guy?' on Venice Pier echoes Faludi's account of 'men's predicament' at the end of *Stiffed*, in that traditional forms of masculinity that used to hold power are now stigmatised as 'oppressive', while men are disbarred from copying the empowering strategies and mechanisms previously used by other identity groups.

Having outlined these wider historical contexts, it is time to locate *Falling Down* in cinema history, especially in relation to what was happening to representations of masculinity and racial whiteness in American cinema in the late 1980s and early 1990s.

Fatherhood Movies and the 'Privilege of Gentleness'

> [T]he image of the sensitive man calls up, for me, the male person
> who, while enjoying the position of unbelievable privilege, also has
> the privilege of gentleness. – Donna Haraway (cited in Jeffords, 1994,
> pp. 206–207)

In the symptomatically titled 1988 essay 'The Forward March of Men
Halted', Rowena Chapman and Jonathan Rutherford noted a relative
decline in men's social and economic status, and the cultural prominence of
the 'new man' and of diverse racial and sexual identities that seemed to put
at stake the previous normative ideal of heterosexual white masculinity. As a
result, according to Chapman and Rutherford

> The masculinity that once believed itself to be at the pinnacle of the
> natural hierarchy of things is now being slowly exposed for what it
> is: a subjectivity that is organised within structures of control and
> authority…For men who were promised recognition and a secure
> place in the world, there lies ahead a frightening prospect: that mascu-
> linity will be shorn of its hierarchical power and will become simply one
> identity among others. (1988, p. 11)

In the late 1980s and early 1990s, the popular cultural debates over
masculinity epitomised by *Newsweek*'s article on 'white male paranoia'
were paralleled by developments in film criticism which revisited its
dependence on psychoanalytical theories of identity. Works such as Kaja
Silverman's *Male Subjectivity at the Margins* (1992) saw itself as very much
within the tradition of psychoanalytical film theory, but broke with the
rigid application of the Freudian heterosexual gender binary, finding much
more dynamism and flexibility than is apparent in the founding texts (see
especially Mulvey, 1975/1989 and Neale, 1983). Later work, including
Collins, Radner, and Collins's *Film Theory Goes to the Movies*, Cohan

and Hark's *Screening the Male*, and Kirkham and Thumim's *You Tarzan: Masculinity, Movies and Men* (all, like *Falling Down*, appearing in 1993), Kirkham and Thumim's slightly later *Me Jane: Masculinity, Movies and Women* (1995), and Lynne Segal's wider-ranging *Slow Motion: Changing Masculinities, Changing Men* (1990), moved still further away from directly psychoanalytical approaches, ranging across star criticism and concerns with ethnicity, 'race', sexuality, and performance, and rethinking Lacanian and post-Lacanian concerns with specularity and gender by detailed reference to national cinemas in the United States, Britain, and India. At the same time, film masculinity became a major focus for critics who saw cinema as one of several cultural arenas in which representations of identity were shifting in significant and interesting ways. Much of this work was clearly positioned as feminist interventions unmasking the deployment of new forms of masculinity as part of the 1980s and 1990s backlash against feminism (Jeffords, 1989, 1993, 1994; Faludi, 1991/1993; Modleski, 1991; Traube, 1992; Pfeil, 1995).

This latter group of critics highlighted the importance of a series of films released in the late 1980s and early 1990s that seemed to respond to the 'crisis of [straight] white masculinity' (Pfeil, 1995, pp. ix, 213, 225–245) and were significant precursors to *Falling Down*. This group includes *Parenthood* (1989), *Uncle Buck* (1989), *Regarding Henry* (1991), *The Fisher King* (1991), and *Terminator 2: Judgement Day* (1991), and, one might add, the slightly later *Groundhog Day* (1993). These were dubbed by Susan Jeffords (1993) the 'male transformation movies'. Each of these films responded to the questioning or weakening of traditional forms of 'hard' masculinity by having their protagonists embrace qualities of nurturing and domesticity that had traditionally been gendered as feminine. Yet in these films, the giving up of what had been defined as authoritative forms of masculinity is in no way a giving up of authority itself. In fact, the reverse: 'feminine' qualities are appropriated as a means of shoring up male power. As Fred Pfeil argued, the hero of what he calls the 'sensitive guy' movies of 1991 is not interested in giving up or sharing power, but instead emerges 'from a temporary, tonic power shortage as someone more deserving of its possession and more compassionate in its exercise' (1995, p. 49). Furthermore, as Elizabeth Traube pointed out in her discussion of *Parenthood*, the ability of male protagonists such as Gil (Steve Martin) to juggle work and domestic worlds is contrasted with the experience of female characters who find that they must choose either career or maternity. What the movie accomplishes is to extend the notion of 'parenthood' from the domestic into the economic sphere – something for which feminist criticism had been arguing for some time – whilst at the same time redefining the male as the appropriate gender to fulfil this dual responsibility. Traube's point is reinforced in her reading of *Uncle Buck*, which performs very similar ideological work in a somewhat different register. In John Hughes's film, Buck (John Candy) is a transgressive, disruptive blue-collar male in the middle-class home, but he humanises the somewhat isolated members of the middle-class family before himself submitting to the disciplines of work and marriage at the end of the film.

It did not escape critics such as Traube, Modleski, Jeffords, and Pfeil that the so-called crisis of straight white masculinity served to keep heterosexual white males centre stage. In short, these critics persuasively regarded Hollywood's 'new men' of the late 1980s and early 1990s as doing powerful cultural work, resisting and defusing the challenges posed by feminism and forging new forms of masculinity that laid claim to power in new ways. Indeed, the construction of a 'crisis of masculinity' in such films might even work as a means of shoring up the cultural pre-eminence of masculinity.

The 'Crisis of Masculinity' in Gender Theory

Tania Modleski has extended these suspicions about the notion of a 'crisis of masculinity' beyond the immediate context of films to the realm of feminist theory and the project of theorising progressive views of gender. Writing in

1991, Modleski cast a critical eye on recent developments in gender theory
such as the prominence of postmodernism and its breaking with essentialist
forms of identity, and the success of feminists in institutionalising the
critical study of gender within the academy. She focused in particular on the
example of the growing body of work by male academics working in and
alongside feminist traditions of gender theory and criticism. This work offers
important lessons for understanding gender formations in American society
in the late 1980s and early 1990s. Modleski argues there is a tendency in
this emerging criticism to define patriarchy – male power – less as a social
formation subject to challenge and change and more as a psychology that
progressive-thinking men are trying to extirpate. This trajectory reverses
the famous feminist slogan 'the personal is political' and, from a materialist
feminist point of view, there is a danger that in the process social formations
are mystified or privatised. Still, as Modleski argues, this work has launched
useful criticism of a long tradition in American culture whereby 'male
subjectivity works to appropriate "femininity" while oppressing women'. In
such circumstances, the sense of 'crisis' as a means of renewing patriarchal
power structures can be found as much in academic theory as in Hollywood
films:

> [H]owever much male subjectivity may be 'in crisis', as certain
> optimistic feminists are now declaring, we need to consider the extent
> to which male power is actually consolidated through cycles of crisis
> and resolution, whereby men ultimately deal with the threat of female
> power by incorporating it. (1991, p. 7)

This salutary point suggests that we need to evaluate carefully both the
gender politics of constructions of crisis and the sense of the particular
1990s 'crisis of white masculinity' as an epochal event called into being
by the gains of the identity movements. Indeed, as early as 1981 certain
feminists had identified a version of the 'crisis of masculinity' as permanently
occupying a central place in American culture. Nina Baym's influential essay

of that year, 'Melodramas of Beset Manhood', demonstrated how such narratives were intrinsic to American literature and its definition. Baym noted how Lionel Trilling's canon-building 1940 essay 'Reality in America' privileges the work of Edgar Allan Poe, Herman Melville, Nathaniel Hawthorne, and Henry James precisely to the extent to which they embody a model of culture as struggle, conflict, and dialectic. '[I]n any culture ... there are likely to be certain artists who contain a large part of the dialectic within themselves, their meaning and power lying in their contradictions; they contain within themselves, it may be said, the very essence of the culture.' (Trilling, 1940, quoted in Baym, 1981, p. 128). Trilling's immediate purpose is to challenge the literary canon defined by Vernon Parrington, whom Trilling famously regarded as having 'but a limited sense of what constitutes a difficulty' (Trilling, 1940/1950, p. 4). Yet as Baym superbly demonstrates, Trilling's own definition was highly limited in terms of the class, gender, and ethnicity of writing positions from which such cultural tensions could be handled:

> [T]heir membership in the dominant middle-class Anglo-Saxon group – and their modest alienation from it – defined their boundaries, enabling them to 'contain within themselves' the 'contradictions' that in Trilling's view, constitute the 'very essence of the culture'. I will call the literature they produced, which Trilling assesses so highly, a 'consensus criticism of consensus'. (Baym, 1981, p. 129)

Baym's central point is that in Trilling's highly influential conception, claims for American literature as incarnating the essence of the national culture are substantiated precisely by reference to the 'melodramas of beset masculinity' identified with writers and their protagonists from Captain Ahab in Melville's *Moby Dick* to Jay Gatsby, and from James Fenimore Cooper's *The Pioneers* to Jack Kerouac's *On The Road* (1957). Moreover this conception persists across a range of critics and critical positions, many of them politically antagonistic to Trilling. In other words, the literary and cultural dominance of male writers is not simply a matter of gender hegemony, but is reciprocally entwined with a particular conception of national culture.

Baym's work was subsequently developed in several interesting directions, including a consideration of how melodramas of beset African American masculinity differed from those of white men (Brown and Clark, 2003). In many ways Modleski's *Feminism Without Women* updated Baym's argument for the early 1990s and with a wider sense of American culture. Baym also proved prophetic within her field of literary criticism as it responded to the gendered and racial shifts in the academy in the 1970s and 1980s. To take one example, Philip Weinstein's 1992 work on William Faulkner, *Faulkner's Subject: A Cosmos No One Owns*, overtly and deliberately engaged with notions of gendered and racial difference, and sought to reposition Faulkner for a post-identity politics critical context. According to Weinstein, 'we continue to read Faulkner because of the turmoil such supposedly privileged figures [his white male protagonists] undergo, as they seek to regulate, revise or revoke their involuntary (and often incoherent) allegiance to their culture's norms of white male subjectivity' (Weinstein, 1992, p. 82). As Jamie Barlowe (1994) has pointed out, drawing upon both Modleski's warnings and Toni Morrison's influential work on the 'Africanist presence' in American literature, Weinstein valorised Faulkner's modernism by arguing that it unmasked how dominant forms of white masculinity maintained their hegemony through encounters with otherness. Work like Weinstein's may draw upon and incorporate the presence of non-white and female others, both figuratively and by appropriating the critical tools developed by feminists and practitioners of critical 'race' theory, but only to reposition anew white masculinity at the centre in its modernist form. Barlowe points to the circularity whereby the effects of the construction of white male subjectivity on the 'other' are at stake in Weinstein's Faulkner only insofar as they contribute to the construction of white male subjectivity.

Falling Down would fit extremely well the model of American literature that Baym identifies and unmasks, its particular melodramas of beset masculinity (those of D-Fens and Prendergast) dramatising explicitly issues of national importance, shifts in national identity alongside multiculturalism, and a perceived lack of civility in contemporary life. The deeper question posed by Baym and Modleski is how to break with the 'consensus criticism of consensus'. Their work and that of the other critics discussed in this section issues a salutary warning as we seek to understand the 'crisis of white masculinity' and the gendered and racial implications of *Falling Down*: namely that the apparently progressive critical move to analyse white masculinity may itself become complicit with the renewal of its power. Work such as Pfeil's *White Guys* wrestles productively with this dilemma, as we must also try to do.

Whiteness: Marked and Unmarked

Just as masculinity had become a critical focus in the late 1980s, so did white racial identity. There are undoubted parallels between Chapman and Rutherford's sense of increased attention to masculinity as a specific set of identity formations, and Richard Dyer's 1988 observations that:

> Power in contemporary society habitually passes itself off as embodied in the normal as opposed to the superior. This is common to all forms of power, but it works in a particularly seductive way with whiteness, because of the way it seems rooted, in common-sense thought, in things other than ethnic difference. The very terms we use to describe the major ethnic divide presented by Western society, 'black' and 'white' are imported from and naturalised by other discourses. (p. 45)

Dyer went on to condense this argument into the foundational statement of his book-length study *White*: 'As long as race is something only applied to non-white peoples, as long as white people are not racially seen and named, they/we function as a human norm. Other people are raced, we are just people' (Dyer, 1997, p. 1). This was the key insight of critical whiteness studies in the late 1980s and early 1990s: that whiteness derived its power through being unmarked, taken as the universal; how whiteness is, or was, a racial identity that perceives itself as un-racialised, and thereby lays claim to authority. In the early 1990s much critical attention was devoted to this unmarked, quasi-universal formation of whiteness, and by the same token, its constitution by the 'marked' nature of blackness. This work has since been recognised as laying the foundations for our contemporary understanding of 'race' in literary and cultural studies (Hall, 1987, 1991; West, 1990; Morrison, 1992; Delgado and Stefancic, 1997), and film studies (Guerrero, 1993; Snead, 1994; Rhines, 1995, 1996; Willis, 1997; Vera and Gordon, 2003).[11]

These critics grappled with questions that were in some ways similar to those highlighted earlier concerning masculinity. While the quasi-universal nature of whiteness seems to call for critical unmasking and specifying, such a response might itself become complicit with maintaining the position of whiteness at the cultural centre. The study of whiteness was therefore a 'risky' project (Brown, 1999, p. 3), but one necessitated by the wider trajectory of critical 'race' theory. Consider for example Allen L. Woll and Randall M. Miller's historical and bibliographical guide *Ethnic and Racial Images in American Film and Television* (1987), one of the most useful reference works on non-white cultural production. For understandable reasons, Woll and Miller did not recognise as ethnic or racial categories either Anglo-Americans or white, Anglo-Saxon Protestants. Of the ten ethnic and racial identities specified (plus 'Others'), their list is dominated by entries on 'Afro-Americans', which take up 138 pages out of a total of 312. The point is not to argue that WASPs should have been included, which would have been impractical in any case. Rather, as Carol Smith (Davies and Smith, 1997, pp. 51–52) has observed, even a project that attempted to foreground and validate images of non-white ethnic and racial identity apparently could not help but preclude recognition of whiteness as a racial category. And without that acknowledgement, the numerical emphasis on African American representations might also reinforce the status of blackness as the means by which whiteness is defined – that is as the non-marked half of a racial binary, rather than as an ethnicity, which would have required a content of some sort, positioned against multiple others.

Given these difficulties, many critics who analysed white racial identity in the 1990s debated the ultimate aims of their work. Arguing that 'whiteness is a construct or identity almost impossible to separate from racial dominance' (1995, p. 9), Ruth Frankenberg tried to effect that separation, seeking new forms of racial whiteness allied with anti-racism. This position derived in part from Frankenberg's sociological interest in the various ways that individuals formed their identity as white people (Frankenberg, 1993), which led her to emphasise whiteness as a multifaceted 'process'. Others regarded whiteness as utterly inseparable from racial dominance, and argued for its 'abolition' or 'end'. For David Roediger (1994), Noel Ignatiev (Ignatiev and Garvey, 1996) and the 'Race Traitor' group ('treason to whiteness is loyalty to humanity'), Vron Ware (1993, pp. 223–224) and others, the critical analysis of racial whiteness was allied with a political project whereby it is 'dismantled, deconstructed, and consigned to history' (Brown, 1999, p.16).

Just like masculinity in the male transformation/'sensitive guy' movies, at the very moment that whiteness was coming under critical focus, it was also shifting. 'Whiteness has been deeply fissured by the racial conflicts of the post-civil rights period', observed Howard Winant in an influential 1997 article: 'Therefore it has been forced into *re*articulations, *re*presentations, *re*interpretations, of the meaning of race, and perforce, of whiteness' (quoted in Vera and Gordon, 2003, p. 187). As Hernán Vera and Andrew M. Gordon add, these rearticulations 'paradoxically, can only be achieved by conceding dramatic changes in the image of African Americans and other minorities but still reproducing the old image of the heroic white self' (2003, p. 187). *Falling Down* must be understood as one of these rearticulations of whiteness, rather than as a direct reflection of any crisis of white masculinity, and Vera and Gordon direct us some of its key reinterpretations of the meaning of 'race'. The film's depictions of the man protesting at the bank, the family in the Whammyburger, and the teenager who shows D-Fens how to use the rocket launcher, may well be seen as products of a sensibility that 'concedes dramatic changes in the image of African Americans', but, and it is a big 'but', these apparently 'positive images' serve more to tell a story about white racial identity than representing blackness. More debatable is the extent to which *Falling Down* reproduces the old image of the heroic white self, especially the splitting of that self between D-Fens and Prendergast. *Falling Down*'s split and shifting evocations of whiteness might be rather more complex even than Vera and Gordon's paradigm.

Coming to Grips with *Falling Down*

Aside from the question of whether D-Fens is an everyman or icon for angry white males, much about the film undermines any straightforward identification with him. The suggestion of his propensity for domestic violence is clearly alienating. The paralleling of his story with that of Prendergast, the police officer who tracks him, confusingly splits audience identification. In the entire film, the only adult with whom D-Fens experiences any feeling of affinity is an African American protesting at a bank for its alleged racism, while the only person D-Fens deliberately kills is a neo-Nazi whose racist, sexist, and homophobic views of America are anathema to him. As a result, many of the scandalised reactions discussed in Part 2 coexisted with a frustration at being unable to identify the film's ideological affiliation. In turn, the film's resistance to being pinned down ideologically became itself an issue addressed by academics and film theorists.

One of the best academic accounts of *Falling Down*'s ideological slipperiness is offered by Sharon Willis. As she put it, *Falling Down* 'appears to be blaring out a message that it is powerfully intent on *not* claiming'; the film 'seems to think it can bump into some of the ugliest

available ideological positions ... without getting stuck in any one of them'
(1997, p. 19). Nevertheless, taking her cue from the 'glut of signs' (1997,
p. 14) in the film and its general sense of being 'under construction' (the
film title invented by D-Fens for the black youth who helps him with
the rocket launcher), Willis manages to identify a structure that defines
the film's ideological negotiation of identity issues. 'We may understand
Falling Down', she argues, 'as a kind of ideological centrifuge with respect
to multicultural society; that is, it scatters all differences around the
central force field emanating from the white middle-class family man, as
if differences could only be positioned in relation to him and his radically
individual identity' (1997, p. 19). This reading grounds the film's ideological
orientation in its depiction of gender, regarding D-Fens's pathology and
Prendergast's redemption as both being rooted in their relationships with
women (D-Fens's nervous mother and Prendergast's needy wife) and home.
However, nuanced, and at times dazzling, as Willis's reading of the film is,
even this may simplify the viewing experience, repeating the assumption
that audiences identify solely and fully with D-Fens and Prendergast, and
therefore that these figures orientate the film ideologically. Building on
Willis's insights, it is also important to take account of the incomplete,
multiple, and shifting forms of identification discussed at the end of Part 2,
and the trajectories in Hollywood film and film theory summarised earlier.
These suggest that a full understanding of *Falling Down* and its controversy
should take account of several considerations.

First, considering *Falling Down* in relation to the earlier 'male
transformation films' suggests complexities in its depiction of gender and
domesticity. Where these renewed the authority of masculinity by annexing
previously feminised qualities, D-Fens's sheer dysfunctionality as a father
implies weakness rather than moral authority. At the climax of the film,
D-Fens's position as a father is usurped by Prendergast, who asserts his
status by bawling out his wife, punching his colleague, and blowing away
D-Fens, and then proceeds to sit himself beside Adele and to impart
avuncular wisdom to Beth. Prendergast's trajectory might be read as

reiterating the combination of public/economic – 'I'm still a cop' – and domestic power that signifies Gil's super-parenthood in *Parenthood*. However, evidence suggests that audiences are perplexed, rather than satisfied, by the mixed messages sent out by the film at this point, either because they find it difficult to disengage from the self-sacrificial D-Fens, or because of their ambivalence about Prendergast's redemption through violence. Either way, it seems that neither is securely grounded in gender terms in the way that the father figures in the earlier movies are. This suggests two almost entirely contradictory interpretations of *Falling Down* as a representation of a crisis of masculinity. On the one hand, its difference from the male transformation movies might be regarded as a refusal to take advantage of the strategies that those films had used in order to regenerate male power, and even perhaps as an implicit rebuke to them. On the other hand, it could be argued that *Falling Down* simply utilises a different, nonetheless strategic sense of crisis. Its very linkage between a crisis of white masculinity and a crisis of national civility may be best understood in this sense as an updating, post-identity politics, of the 'melodramas of beset masculinity'.

This *strategic* use of a crisis of masculinity has a partial parallel in the film's depiction of white racial identity. From the perspective of critical whiteness studies, it is the complexity of the film's depictions of white racial identity that stand out, with Nick the neo-Nazi occupying an extreme position, Prendergast representing a normative whiteness, and D-Fens oscillating between the two. As Richard Dyer has pointed out, *Falling Down* 'contains the representation of both extreme whiteness, ambivalently perceived, and ordinary whiteness, that is, whiteness as ordinariness' (1997, p. 222). Here we need to understand critically how the film's portrayal of D-Fens might alienate viewers from the pathological elements of white masculinity, even as the film regularly makes us feel sympathy for him. Dyer closes his book *White* with a reading of D-Fens as the embodiment of 'white death' (1997, pp. 217–222); we should make room for a reading of the film as an exposure of the authoritarian elements of patriarchal whiteness, as well as an attempt to reiterate white power.

Third, it is necessary to pay more attention to the sequential structure of the film than most critics have done hitherto. Certain critics, such as Willis, who thinks that 'the film is ultimately more about Prendergast than D-Fens', privilege the narrative closure enacted in D-Fens's death and his supersession as father by Prendergast. Yet audience research of various sorts (Rauzi, 1993; Gabriel, 1996) suggests that people also experience and recall the film as a succession of confrontation scenes. D-Fens's centrality to the overall narrative and his ubiquity in linking each scene substantiate Willis's reading of the film as operating as a kind of 'ideological centrifuge' organising difference around the central position occupied by white masculinity. However there is also a countervailing logic. Within each scene D-Fens's whiteness and masculinity are necessarily performed in relation to others, who need not remain 'Others'. In fact, the structuring of the film into a succession of confrontation scenes ensures that, while viewers perceive D-Fens as the centre of the action throughout, his own experience is one of successive exclusion and marginalisation.

It is to the most significant of these scenes that we now turn.

✖ Part 4

READING *FALLING DOWN*

Interpreting *Falling Down*

Part 2 of this book described the popular controversy surrounding *Falling Down*, and Part 3 outlined two wider contexts: the social and cultural conflicts over identity known as the 'culture wars', and parallel developments in academic discussions of film and identity. At the close of Part 3 we brought these various strands together in order to identify three major issues that determine the significance of *Falling Down*: its depiction of masculinity; its depiction of white racial identity in relation to other ethnic and racial identities; and questions of narrative structure, especially those concerning whether the film is primarily meaningful as a succession of scenes, or if audiences remember above all the narrative closure provided by Prendergast's triumph at the end. This part of the book analyses in detail specific scenes in the light of these issues, building on the interpretations of *Falling Down* that have been made by academic film theorists and critics.

 Falling Down has been recognised as an important film, rather than as a particularly good one, because of its role in moulding popular understandings of 'race' and gender. As Sharon Willis put it, *Falling Down* was one of many early 1990s films that played a role in 'reshaping the public sphere' (1997, p. 7). The film is shot through with an awareness of the politics of identity for which the notion of the culture wars became shorthand. Most strikingly, as we have seen, the film related itself to a 'crisis of white masculinity' (Pfeil, 1995; Davies, 1995a, 1995b; Davies and Smith, 1997). When academic critics came to consider exactly what significance *Falling Down* had with respect to all of this, it is notable that they saw its ambiguities and multiple meanings as posing particular problems of interpretation. Engaged critics often see it as their role to pin down cultural texts with respect to particular ideological positions. Yet here was 'a complex and not completely coherent film' (Davies, 1995a, p. 215) whose incoherence was a crucial part of its significance. Indeed for Pfeil, *Falling Down*'s ambiguity *is* its significance (1995, pp. 238–245). A useful way of addressing this problem, and indeed a corrective to most of the positions in the popular controversy over *Falling Down*, was formulated by John Gabriel on the basis of his research with audience members from various ethnic and racial backgrounds in Birmingham, UK. 'Everyone with whom I spoke', Gabriel wrote, '*identified powerfully, but, importantly, only partially and inconsistently* [emphasis added], with the situations, and, to a lesser extent, with the frustrations, reactions, and point of view of the central character' (1996, p. 134). As Gabriel went on to argue, the fundamental contradictions in the film's depiction of identity, which had been the focus of academic criticism, are not susceptible to a single diagnostic interpretation. Rather, 'the precise ways in which these contradictions are understood depends on reception processes and cultural factors peculiar to specific audiences' (1996, p. 139).

Tracing the *Falling Down* controversy thus far has revealed ample evidence of the different reception processes and cultural factors at work in shaping different audiences', commentators', and critics' views of the film. While individual contributions to that controversy have often tended to narrow down into unitary, diagnostic statements on the model of 'It means this!', the controversy in popular media pointed in different directions and shifted markedly, narrowing the focus onto the figure of D-Fens between the film's US opening in February 1993 and UK release the following June. Therefore it is necessary, when analysing specific scenes in detail, to pay attention both to the theoretical debates over identity representation, and to evidence about the interpretations made by specific audiences and the contexts in which they read the film. Though it is impossible to go back to *Falling Down*'s release to generate new audience research, a range of audience interpretations and identifications can be gleaned from John Gabriel's research among viewers in Britain and from aspects of the 1993 coverage in US media. Finally, it is important to acknowledge the influence exerted upon audience reactions by the marked similarities between certain scenes in the film and widely shown or debated media coverage of actual news stories. As we saw in Part 1, *Falling Down* was conceived by its screenwriter and director in relation to television news stories, and as we saw in Part 2, certain audiences read D-Fens as a fictionalised counterpart to the real-life figure Bernhard Goetz, and in conjunction with media coverage associated with the Los Angeles riots. These associations inevitably shaped interpretations of the film, and *Falling Down* must therefore be understood as being in some ways intertextually entwined with these 'media events' of urban violence.

Jammed In

The opening scene of *Falling Down* is in many ways the whole film in miniature: a micro-version of the 'average man who just happened to break' narrative, a crystallisation of its double game of portraying the white male as both typically and especially frustrated by the contemporary United States. The first frames are a close-up of a mouth, identifiable as the camera moves back as that of a white male (Michael Douglas). The scene is a traffic jam, emblematic of anyone's workaday frustrations. The camera cuts between a range of faces stuck in this same boat: Caucasian, Latina/o, black, male, female, middle-aged, very young (children on a school bus), and even feline (a car-window decoration in the shape of Garfield the cartoon cat). A woman uses her door mirror to put on lipstick. A Latina girl and her cuddly toys stare fixedly from the car in front. Two men in an open-top sports car argue into a mobile telephone. The first face appears with increasing frequency; it is that of a white male in a white shirt and tie, with a buzz cut and glasses only one step more stylish than aviator frames. He gradually loses his cool as his car's air conditioning fails and then its window handle breaks off in his hand. The tension builds with quick cuts between the construction signs, the woman putting on lipstick, bumper stickers, Garfield, and the children in the school bus, until the Douglas character cracks, stepping out of his car and picking his way through stationary traffic to the side of the freeway. Asked by an irate motorist where the hell he thinks he is going, he replies, 'I'm going home' before running off into the distance.[12]

This as yet unnamed white male is thus marked out as the film's protagonist, and as epitomising the notion that white males have it the same as everyone else, only worse. After he has gone, a middle-aged man (Robert Duvall) persuades a rather fussy traffic cop to help push the abandoned car off the road, which they do with the help of another motorist who turns out to be a linoleum tile salesman. Duvall identifies himself as Prendergast, a police officer on the way to his last day at the Robbery Division downtown before retirement.

It is Prendergast whose attention is arrested by two more signs among the many in the scene; the personalised licence plate of the abandoned car, D-FENS, and a large hoarding by the side of the freeway advertising Hawaiian Tropic sunscreen (see Figure 1). It shows a woman in a bikini with the caption 'White Is For Laundry'. Deprived of their commodity referent, the words invoke some sort of racial taunt. A graffiti artist has drawn a cartoon man trapped between the woman's breasts, with a speech bubble saying 'HELP!!' As well as making explicit the 'white masculinity in crisis' theme, the hoarding will later serve as a marker for Prendergast, enabling him to identify the white guy running amok across Los Angeles as the one whose car he pushed off the highway.

Sharon Willis shows how this opening scene sets up the film by disrupting and restabilising the ways that audiences make sense of it. She points out that the initial close-up view of D-Fens through a fish-eye lens makes us view him through a distorted perspective that echoes his own. The intercutting of scenes of D-Fens with the contextualising shots, presumably from his perspective (we look up at the children, who are looking down from the school bus), foregrounds what Willis sees as the deep ideological structure of the film, its scattering of difference around the centred white male figure. For her the scene is also symptomatic of the film as a whole in another way. As Willis puts it, 'the opening sequence takes pains to establish the fact that we cannot establish where the problem of interpretation lies. Are the signs themselves fragmentary and unreliable, or is it the reader's perspective?' (1997, p. 15). By this Willis is referring to the processes by which the film disguises or confuses its meaning – what we have called its ambiguity – so that the scene both foregrounds the plight of the white male yet also undermines his perspective. Undoubtedly D-Fens is feeling the bedlam of a multicultural America rave around him, but this scene fails to make it clear whether audiences should feel this too – in fact it deliberately confuses and multiplies our viewing positions. In the end, for Willis, it will be Prendergast, or more specifically, the paralleling of D-Fens's confusions with Prendergast's, and the latter's resolution of them in the final reel, that ultimately grounds the film's depiction of white masculinity. But not yet.

That the scene itself leaves this unresolved is hardly surprising – it is a source of narrative tension. But it is worth considering how far the scene goes in refusing to allow audiences to orientate themselves with respect to the protagonists. None of the four men at the centre of the scene elicits strong audience identification. D-Fens already appears somewhat unhinged, the linoleum tile salesman (a cameo by screenwriter Ebbe Roe Smith) is oleaginous, and the traffic cop is officious. The scene closes in comedy at the expense of two of these characters, as the cop's cherished motorcycle falls over and he goes to pick it up, leaving the salesman stuck behind D-Fens's car and trying to prevent it rolling back on to the freeway. The cop's name, according to his badge, is 'Bobbit', which would have a particular significance for viewers in the light of a June 1993 news story from Virginia detailing how one Lorena Bobbit cut off the penis of her husband with a carving knife and threw it from the window of her car. Even without this association, Officer Bobbit's ostentatious sunglasses and over-anxiety about his gleaming motorcycle poke fun at what Susan Faludi would later call 'ornamental' masculinity, glamorous images of manhood that lay claim to the trappings of male power while its essence is ebbing away (1999, pp. 505–508, 598–600). All of which leaves the moustached, balding, and retiring Prendergast as the most likely, or rather, least unlikely, figure for audience identification.

Mr Lee's Store

D-Fens's encounter with the Korean shopkeeper (Figure 3) from 07:47 to 12:23 was received as one of the most provocative aspects of *Falling*

Figure 3:   First view of Mr Lee, the Korean shopkeeper.

Down. Objections focused primarily on the stereotypical depiction of the shopkeeper, who speaks heavily accented English and rudely refuses to provide D-Fens with change to make a telephone call, and on the violence that D-Fens metes out to his displays at the end of the scene, outraged by the shop's high prices, epitomised by 85 cents for a can of Coca Cola.[13]

With his hands in an old-fashioned cashier's till (cashbox), a cigarette between his lips, his face unshaven, and frequently scratching his stomach, Mr Lee is every inch a stereotype: the villainous shopkeeper or barman of the classic Western movie. He exudes rudeness, mistrust, and suspicion, culminating in his producing a baseball bat from behind the counter. In Western fashion too, D-Fens turns the weapon against him. But if the shopkeeper's eyes are narrowed in suspicion of D-Fens as he enters the store, they also disclose an unpleasant ethnic stereotype of Korean shopkeepers 'as rude, money-grubbing menaces', as Jeana Park (1993) of the Korean American Advocates for Justice argued during the *Falling Down* controversy. Park's primary concern was that the depiction of the shopkeeper reinforced a negative stereotype of the aggressive Korean shopkeeper that was already in circulation, stirring up racial tensions and leading to 'hate crimes and violence against us'. 'It was this stereotype' Park argued,

> that helped fuel the tensions between African Americans and Korean
> Americans for years. Recall how the case of Soon Ja Du was so widely
> heralded as an example of this war, and recall how that incident was
> so exploited that just the name Latasha Harlins became a focal point
> for an all-out attack on the Korean American community. We Korean
> Americans were targeted, attacked and suffered the brunt of the
> damages during last year's civil unrest. And the violence continues,
> with Korean American store owners being victims of assault and hate
> crimes almost every day. (1993)

Park's claims were paralleled by reports suggesting that attacks on and
robberies from Korean-owned business continued alongside the film's
release (Baker, 1993). Unlike in the case of *A Clockwork Orange* (1971),
there were no specific charges that the film had inspired copycat incidents.
Rather, *Falling Down* was viewed intertextually with other media spectacles
of racialised violence as inflaming an already tense situation. Jeana Park's
reference to the Soon Ja Du/Latasha Harlins case is instructive. That case
has long been seen as contributing to the tensions that erupted in April
1992, and this is how *Time* magazine reported the incident on the fifteenth
anniversary of the riots:

> In many ways, the shooting death of 15-year-old Latasha Harlins on
> March 16, 1991 by convenience store clerk Soon Ja Du, a Korean
> immigrant, laid the foundation of anger and resentment that would
> eventually explode after the [Rodney] King verdict. On the afternoon
> of March 16, 1991, the 15-year-old Harlins entered the Empire Liquor
> Market, which was owned by Du's family. Harlins put a $1.79 bottle of
> orange juice in her bag and, security cameras showed, approached
> the counter with money in her hand. Du didn't see the money, however,
> and confronted Harlins over what she saw as an attempted theft. After
> a brief scuffle, Harlins left the orange juice on the counter and started
> to leave, only to be shot in the back of the head by Du. (Singal, 2007)

At her trial, Du claimed that the gun had gone off by mistake. On 15 November 1991, she was convicted of voluntary manslaughter, but avoided a prison sentence, instead being placed on probation, fined, and ordered to perform 400 hours community service. Amid protests from black community leaders, Los Angeles District Attorney Ira Reiner called the case a 'terrible miscarriage of justice' and removed the judge involved from criminal cases. Nevertheless, a poor quality video recording of the incident, made by the store's security camera and widely shown on television, made an equally inflammatory twin to that of the Rodney King beating.

The scene in *Falling Down* might be regarded as replaying several aspects of the incident in a provocative fashion. A strong interpretation of both incidents views the shopkeepers as mis-reading the situation because of their excessively suspicious attitude. At the end of the scene, D-Fens pointedly puts the can of coca cola on the counter and leaves 50 cents in the till to pay for it, in a way that parallels and in a way reproachfully completes Harlins's action in leaving the orange juice on the counter.

Park's article (1993) makes two further significant points. One of the few contributors to the popular controversy to broach the issue of audiences' split identifications, she contests the notion that they are distanced from D-Fens, arguing that while viewers 'may not condone his violence' they nevertheless 'understand his anger and frustration'. Perhaps her most telling criticism is made in the form of an anecdote:

> I was talking about this movie with a friend of mine who asked me, 'Would it have been any different if the store owner was an American?' Oh God, I felt as if a vein burst in my forehead. 'That is exactly my point!' I wanted to scream at her, 'He is an American! Get it through your head! Mr. Lee is an American just like you!'

We have suggested earlier that D-Fens in this scene arrogates American history to his own identity; in 'rolling back prices to 1965' he evinces a desire

to return to an America imagined to be unproblematically white. When
D-Fens asks 'Do you know how much money my country has given your
country?' and Mr Lee replies smartly 'How much?', D-Fens is at a loss to
answer; while this implies that his resentment has murky origins in racial
prejudice, it also leaves no room for a sense that Mr Lee is just as 'American'
as he is. When Mr Lee accepts D-Fens's distinction between 'my country'
and 'your country', Park implies, he accepts D-Fens's racial definition of
who really is American, and with it his own relegation to second-class
citizenship.

     Particularly when considered in the immediate context of the riots,
the scene's intertextual relationship with the video of the Du/Harlins
incident also raises the question of D-Fens's symbolic relationship
with blackness. Peter Rainer's critique of the film in the *L.A. Times* had
pointed out that the 'conspicuously few' African American characters
in the film were all 'haloed', and wondered: 'Is it too cynical to suggest
that the Korean merchant in this film was included as a sop to the
animosities of the commercially imposing black audience' (Rainer, 1993).
Notwithstanding such calculations, the symbolic weight attached to
African American characters noted by Rainer suggests that *Falling Down*
is engaged in the kinds of 're-articulation' of white/African American
relations identified by critics such as Winant, and Vera and Gordon (and
discussed in Part 3). At one level, D-Fens is presented here in the terms
that Vera and Gordon suggest have characterised white heroes in relation
to blacks throughout twentieth-century film and that persist in post-
identity politics films such as *Amistad* (1997). Like such 'sincere fictions
of the saviour', D-Fens might almost be read here as a 'messianic white
self, the redeemer of the weak' (Vera and Gordon, 2003, p. 3) avenging
Latasha Harlins, or even as a parody of such a redeeming figure. More
covertly, alongside D-Fens's 'standing up for my rights as a consumer'
crusade against inflation and profiteering, the scene begins the figuration
of an implicit bond between D-Fens and African Americans, which
will be cemented later on with the black protester, the young boy in the

Whammyburger, and the black youth who explains how to use the rocket launcher. Such black/white bonds are not uncommon in late 1980s and early 1990s films, and can be seen perhaps most obviously in the bi-racial buddy movies epitomised by the *Lethal Weapon* series (1987–1998), as well as in Lawrence Kasdan's *Grand Canyon* (1991), but in its particular re-articulation of 'race', *Falling Down* provocatively adds to this the overtly negative characterisations of other ethnic minorities; not only the Korean shopkeeper but also Latino gang members.

While few British audience members would have been familiar with the Soon Ja Du/Latasha Harlins case, several of John Gabriel's interviewees criticised D-Fens's racial/national rhetoric in ways that paralleled the reactions of Jeana Park and other Korean Americans who contributed vox pops to the *Los Angeles Times* (Rauzi, 1993). Though some initially sympathised with D-Fens's frustrations, Gabriel reports that by the end of the scene 'what united my interviewees was their almost unanimous condemnation of an act of racism' (1996, p. 141). Moreover at least three of his interviewees recognised and rejected D-Fens's racialised definition of American history. As one, 'Bill', put it:

> Why [D-Fens] wanted to go back to 1965, not because the prices were lower, but because he (the Korean) didn't own the corner shop and he didn't tell him (D-Fens) what the prices were. It was going back to another age when there hadn't been an enormous influx of Asian immigration into America. (1996, p. 142)

For Gabriel the course of the scene not only played out the ways that audience's identifications split and shifted throughout the film, but also his finding that most viewers tended to be sympathetic to D-Fens when he occupied 'universal' situations, and alienated from him when he was most identified as 'white'.

The Drive-by

The drive-by scene takes up a little over five minutes of the film, between 24:20 and 29:45. As in the film as a whole, the main focus of this section is on D-Fens, but his narrative is intercut with scenes featuring Prendergast in the police station and Beth at home. Having escaped the attentions of the two Latino gang members on the hill, D-Fens is still in a Latino area, as the myriads of Spanish-language signs, graffiti, stickers, and murals that surround him proclaim. The largest and most striking sign belongs to an old cinema which has been converted into a shop, called 'La Barata' ('cheap' in Spanish). Outside La Barata (Figure 4) D-Fens calls Beth again on a public telephone, announcing his very unwelcome intention of calling at her house to see his daughter on her birthday. He is spotted by the gang members upon whose 'territory' he had trespassed earlier, and they decide to shoot him.

From the beginning to the end of this scene, the contest between D-Fens and the gang members is portrayed in highly racialised terms as a clash between contrasting identities, white and Latino. The gang members'

Figure 4:　Outside La Barata.

appearance and actions are stereotyped. Much of their upper bodies are exposed, revealing extensive tattoos. They gesture wildly; they talk loudly and argue between themselves; they are excitable; they are violent. The contrast with D-Fens is extreme. Where the gang members are tattooed, no doubt signifying some kind of gang affiliation, his white shirt is the epitome of blankness. His pressed, clean appearance contrasts also with the surroundings of this obviously Latino neighbourhood which, like the gang members' bodies, is extensively inscribed with Spanish-language signs, graffiti, and murals.

In contrast to Latino volubility and excitability, D-Fens is calm throughout. He moves very slowly and talks in a low voice (as does Beth on the other end of the telephone) even when the two of them are arguing over his plan to visit her house. Of course there is not just one set of racial stereotypes in play here, but two. It is just that the stereotype of white racial identity embodied by D-Fens is normally unmarked.

The narrative organisation of the scene confirms these stereotypes, bearing out the correctness, as it were, of judging from appearances. This narrative is initiated and defined by the gang members losing control of themselves. Already discussing excitedly their encounter with the white guy, when they see D-Fens they lose all restraint. The sole female in the car, whose name is later revealed as Angie (Karina Arroyave), attempts to moderate their behaviour by asking the four young men to think of the possible repercussions of their actions. 'He's not worth it', she says, referring to D-Fens. Their response is to shout her down and to eject her from the car. They then pull out their weapons, preparing to shoot D-Fens as he talks to Beth on the telephone. Opening fire, they are so excited that they somehow miss him completely, instead covering several storefronts in a hail of bullets and wounding, apparently fatally, several bystanders. Finally, in their confusion over whether they have hit him, they crash the car. In complete contrast, D-Fens remains still and inexpressive throughout. He hardly reacts to the deluge of bullets, as glass shatters, bystanders stagger and fall, and twice the camera tracks so quickly that all we can see is a blur.

As D-Fens lifts his briefcase from the top of the telephone stand and turns, the film goes into slow motion, although this is barely noticeable as we are already accustomed to D-Fens moving slowly. Picking his way through shooting victims and people rushing to help them, he walks purposefully (and bravely?) in the direction of the crashed car. Once there, again he speaks quietly and moves slowly. He points out that they had missed him, and picks up and fires a semi-automatic. The bullet ricochets harmlessly off the car. He reloads and takes aim again, while the only gang member still conscious pleads for mercy. The camera frames D-Fens and the gun against the sky. At the last moment D-Fens adjusts the angle of fire and shoots the gang member in the leg.

This short sequence recalls the famous 'Do you feel lucky, punk?' sequence from the Clint Eastwood action thriller *Dirty Harry* (1971). There, Eastwood, as Police Inspector Harry Callahan, stands over an African American bank robber (Albert Popwell) and challenges him to take a chance on his having fired all six shots from his revolver. Eastwood's performance in that scene is similarly slowly paced, and even exaggerated, in its mannered coolness. In comparison, Douglas performs D-Fens as struggling to keep control (Figure 5).

Figure 5:   D-Fens as (Dirty) Harry Callahan.

Turning away, D-Fens mutters: 'Get some shooting lessons, asshole', fills the gym bag with guns from the car and walks off across the street slowly and sedately. Angie, the young Latina previously ejected from the car, runs past him screaming and gesturing wildly, elbows akimbo, her hands up to her face. Again, the contrast is striking (Figure 6).

As D-Fens walks off down the sidewalk, the camera follows him and closes in on what he is carrying – the briefcase in one hand and the gym bag full of guns in the other.

Robin Rauzi's *Los Angeles Times* article (1993) describes an exchange over the 'accuracy' of this scene between Carrie Walker and her husband, Patrick, of South Pasadena.

> 'I guess the Hispanic gang members (were stereotyped)', Carrie said. 'It seemed awfully over-dramatized, him swearing at his girlfriend ...'
>
> 'But in that group – I mean, that's an accurate portrayal of that group', Patrick countered.
>
> 'I've never ridden in a car with them', she said. 'I don't know. Seriously, it's Hollywood.'
>
> 'It's not just Hollywood', he said. 'It's reality.'

Figure 6:   D-Fens and Angie cross.

This brief conversation condenses what has become a familiar debate about negative stereotyping and accuracy in Hollywood movies. Symptomatically, the discussion as reported by Rauzi perceives the issue of stereotyping only in relation to Latino 'race'/ethnicity. In a way this is not surprising, as the scene overtly plays to negative stereotypes of Latinos in ways that explicitly call up some of the most authoritarian aspects of the thriller genre from *Dirty Harry* to *Death Wish* and that remind us that the targeting of marginal figures was normalised in films from the late 1960s and early 1970s, 'where hippies, Vietnam vets, black drug dealers, white drug dealers, bleeding-heart liberals, cops and the press were all regularly whacked' (Rainer, 1993). Less obviously, in the extreme contrast between Latino and white enforced throughout the scene, can we see something that Carrie and Patrick seem not to have seen? Can we see the marking of D-Fens's whiteness? As critical white studies was pointing out at the time, white racial identity long derived its power, in parallel with masculinity, through being unmarked, the norm, unnoticed, taken for granted; in a word, blank. Here however the extreme contrast with the Latinos throws into relief the signs of whiteness. The effect might be, if not quite to see whiteness from the outside, then at least to defamiliarise whiteness, to make viewers aware of the composition of white racial identity as image and performance, something that had up until this point tended to remain invisible, or at least unremarked upon, in mainstream (that is, white dominated) American culture.

D-Fens's cold-blooded cruelty lays bare a pathological element in whiteness with which non-whites in colonial societies are all too familiar, but which is seldom perceived by whites, and indeed thereby functions as a means of maintaining white power. Read through the understanding of 'race' disseminated by Frantz Fanon's *Black Skin, White Masks*, D-Fens throws into relief this colonial discourse of 'race'. Walking off down the street with a bag of guns in one hand and a briefcase (which will turn out to be empty, except for a packed lunch) in the other, he exposes the pathological meaning of whiteness, a pathology all the more chilling for its association with calm and even vacancy.[14]

This scene was one of the few occasions in *Falling Down* when (self)-censorship became an issue. According to the film's editor Paul Hirsch, after early preview screenings Warner Bros asked that D-Fens's cold-blooded shooting of the gang member in the leg be taken out. When the re-cut film was subsequently shown to a second preview audience, Hirsch explains, this had the effect of robbing the final scene of much of its tension for a significant number of viewers, as they did not believe that D-Fens would shoot Prendergast. The earlier shot therefore fulfilled a significant function in signalling to viewers that D-Fens 'is crazy, he may do anything, he's not bound by the laws of society as you and I understand them' (Hirsch, commentary track, Schumacher, 1993/2009). The studio subsequently allowed the cut to be reinstated.

Hirsch's reading of D-Fens's calmness as implying that he inhabits a 'crazy' space outside society may hold true for some viewers, but the scene may also be read in a completely opposite fashion. D-Fens's utter calm throughout the scene might also imply a confidence that he is beyond the reach of the law. The scene might therefore be read as exposing the privileges and self-confidence of a pathological whiteness whose fantasy version is offered by thrillers like *Death Wish* and *Dirty Harry*, and whose reality was tested in such judicial/media events as the trials of the LAPD officers who beat Rodney King, and the 1986–1987 trial of Bernhard Goetz. It will be remembered that Goetz's case was recalled several times during the *Falling Down* controversy (for example Ansen, 1993, p. 80; Hinson, 1993; the *Crossfire* programme), and it is this scene that most closely parallels the incident for which Goetz became famous. On 22 December 1984, Goetz, a 37-year-old self-employed electrical engineer, was travelling on the New York subway when he was approached by several black teenagers, Troy Canty, Barry Allen, James Ramseur, and Darell Cabey, one of whom asked him for five dollars, and when he refused, demanded: 'Give us your money'. Fearing that he was about to be mugged, Goetz drew a concealed, unlicensed revolver and opened fire, wounding all four. He subsequently went on the run, during which time media coverage of the 'subway vigilante' made him something of a popular hero to New Yorkers suffering a legendarily high level of violent crime. Eight days after the shooting Goetz gave himself up to police in Concord, New Hampshire, and made a confession. After much legal wrangling, he was tried between December 1986 and June 1987 on 13 charges, ranging from possessing an unlicensed firearm to attempted murder. Goetz was found guilty of only one charge, 'criminal possession of a weapon in the third degree', and later sentenced to a six-month jail term, alongside several non-custodial sanctions.

Goetz's high public profile and the assumption made later in the film by the neo-Nazi storekeeper that D-Fens is a 'vigilante' suggest general parallels, but the drive-by scene also links D-Fens with what proved to be a crucial part of the incident, much discussed at Goetz's trial. Goetz fired five shots in all. The first three injured Canty, Allen, and Ramseur, and the fourth, at Cabey, missed. It was the fifth and final shot that hit Cabey while the latter was sitting on one of the seats in the subway carriage. As a result he almost died, ending up severely paralysed. Goetz's trial for attempted murder turned on interpretations of this fifth shot. His defence portrayed all five shots as belonging to one sequence, made in one panicky gesture of self-defence, while the prosecution argued that the fifth shot was an offensive action undertaken in cold blood. This was evidenced by witness statements, and by the confession Goetz had made to police, which described him as pausing after the fourth shot, going over to Cabey, and saying – or at least thinking, 'You don't look so bad, here's another!', before shooting him at point blank range. In 1996 a civil trial awarded $43 million in damages to the still paralysed Cabey. Goetz immediately declared himself bankrupt.

Whatever its importance in building tension in the final scene of the film, and there is no reason to doubt Hirsch's account, D-Fens's final shot at the gang member cannot help but suggest a link between whiteness and pathological violence, an association all the more frightening due to his apparent calm. The echoes of the Bernhard Goetz and Rodney King cases suggest that, at exactly the same time that D-Fens embodies an extreme, pathological whiteness, one which might itself be feared and abhorred by certain audiences or be the subject of fantasised identification by others, he also incarnates whiteness in a much more 'ordinary' position of legal privilege.

'Not Economically Viable'

Of course a salient difference between the drive-by scene and the Goetz and King cases is the racial/ethnic identity of the white males' victims. In substituting Latinos for the African Americans of those cases, the drive-by scene expands on the racial logic established earlier in Mr Lee's store; one that positions whites and blacks alongside one another in antagonism to other ethnic groups. The most positive evocation of this link is made in the short scene following the Whammyburger incident, which features Vondie Curtis-Hall as a protester picketing a bank for its alleged racism (Figure 7). Never named in the film (the credits refer to him as 'Not Economically Viable Man'), the protester wears similar clothes to D-Fens, a white shirt and tie, and dark trousers.

Figure 7:   Echoes of the Civil Rights movement (Vondie Curtis-Hall).

The protester holds a sign saying 'Not Economically Viable', presumably the explanation given by the bank for refusing him a loan, which he suspects is a form of coded racism. As D-Fens approaches, he points to a white male leaving the bank, commenting ironically that this man must be 'economically viable'. D-Fens looks at the protester long and hard, then goes into a cheap store across the street to buy a unicorn snow globe as a birthday present for his daughter. When he comes out, the protester is being taken away in a police car. Their eyes meet and through the window of the police cruiser the protester says, 'Don't forget me'. D-Fens nods slightly in acknowledgement.

Cross-racial male friendships have been a salient feature of American culture since at least as far back as the first appearance of Chingachook, the last of the Mohicans, and the white trapper known as Leatherstocking in James Fenimore Cooper's 1823 novel *The Pioneers*. Resonant examples include Huck Finn and Jim the escaped slave in Mark Twain's 1885 classic *The Adventures of Huckleberry Finn*, and were famously re-enacted in the beats' relationship with jazz, as in Jack Kerouac's *On The Road*. Critics have argued that more often than not such non-white figures and cultural forms act as a symbolic means of exploring the liminal forms of white masculinity (see for example Kennedy, 2000, p. 39). 'In America', as the historian of 'race' and ethnicity Werner Sollors has remarked, 'casting oneself as an outsider may in fact be considered a dominant trait' (1986, p. 31); and a frequent part of that casting has been to annex certain elements, if not the marginal position, of non-whites. In order for this symbolic appropriation of non-white identity to work, such texts tend to decouple the cultural and symbolic power possessed by the racial other from any political understanding of 'race'.

In *Falling Down*'s version, exactly the opposite of this decoupling seems to be happening. Dressed as he is, and with his placard, the black protester is a figure who explicitly references the civil rights movement and, with it, the politicisation of 'race'. Even so, some critics have argued that this politicised racial history is brought up by the film only to be erased by being equated with D-Fens's condition. This sense of a double movement of historical reference and erasure informs how cultural critic Liam Kennedy reads the scene: 'The gaze between the two men', Kennedy argues,

> is presented as one of equal recognition … However, given the privileges accorded D-Fens' imperial vision throughout the film his gaze can only function to colonize and determine the meanings of 'blackness'. The crude liberalism motivating this scene at once idealises and negates the alterity of the black subject. More than this, it induces historical amnesia. (1996, p. 96)

Kennedy is surely right to suggest that the protester functions primarily to help define D-Fens, and that if the two men's conditions are to be equated, the oppression of African Americans is dehistoricised. In this sense, the figure of the protester clearly exemplifies Vera and Gordon's point that 'the new images [of identity] apparently recognize the humanity of minority groups but actually misrecognize the true relations between minorities and whites' (2003, p. 187). However, it is worth reflecting further on this act of mis-recognition, where it takes place and how the film situates it, bearing in mind what has been said about audiences' split and shifting identification with D-Fens.

Complicating the bond between them, the protester's evident affiliation with a racial tradition of protest functions as a counterpoint to D-Fens. The protester's appearance and actions suggest that he possesses an awareness of civil rights history that gives him both an understanding of his current situation, as someone who has been victimised by racism, and a means of responding articulately and with some power. Moreover, because his racial identity is overtly politicised, any 'authenticity' connoted by his blackness cannot be transferred across racial lines. The protester therefore functions iconically in complete contrast to the ways in which black figures were used in classic American literature, signalling a lack in whiteness that cannot be made up. That lack is D-Fens's conspicuous inability to understand his own position, a lack thrown into relief by their similar appearance. D-Fens's embrace of the 'universal' notion of whiteness becomes *his* problem, *his* deficit, a block to *his* understanding. He embodies in racial as well as gendered terms the 1990s condition of 'stiffed' masculinity that Susan Faludi describes:

> The male paradigm is peculiarly unsuited to mounting a challenge to men's predicament. Men have no clearly defined enemy who is oppressing them. How can men be oppressed when the culture has already identified them as oppressors, and when they see themselves that way? As one man wrote plaintively to Promise Keepers, 'I'm like a kite with a broken string, but I'm also holding the tail.' (1999, p. 604)

Under such circumstances, we may well ask whether the look between them is one of 'equal recognition', or if, as seems equally plausible, D-Fens remains in a state of confusion, and his identification with the protester is as partial and fleeting as is audiences' identification with him.

Later, on Venice Pier, D-Fens will use the black protester's terminology to explain himself to Prendergast. 'I'm not…economically viable', he says, explaining that he used to build missiles. Of course this is a fundamental mis-recognition, in that the protester had been employing the term ironically, suggesting that the bank used it when the real reason for denying him a loan was racial prejudice. But it is far from clear that audiences make the same mis-recognition, nor even that the film invites them to.[15]

'What Kind of Vigilante Are You?'

At 55:12 D-Fens enters a military surplus store in search of hiking boots to replace his shoes, which have holes in the soles. The ensuing encounter with the store's owner, a homophobic neo-Nazi who taunts D-Fens sexually before D-Fens stabs him in self-defence and then shoots him dead, generates a surplus of signification around violence, whiteness, masculinity, and sexuality, that makes the scene one of the most complex of the film.

Nick, the store owner (Frederic Forrest), recognises D-Fens from the
description of the Whammyburger incident to which he has been listening
on his police scanner. Nick seemingly tries to impress D-Fens by harassing
a couple of gay men who are shopping in his store, recommending some
jungle boots that have seen service in Vietnam and are 'great for stomping
queers'. When one of the gay men confronts him, he pulls out a gun;
meanwhile D-Fens has sidled off to look at some other boots. Nick then
helps to conceal D-Fens from Officer Sandra Torres, who enters the shop
while taking part in the police search of the area. D-Fens is more than
usually quiet and looks strangely vulnerable. Nick takes him into a dark back
room full of Nazi memorabilia, shows him a container of Zyklon B that
was 'actually used' to gas Jews, and gives him a portable rocket launcher to
help in his vigilante activity, all along using deeply racist and homophobic
language. D-Fens eventually explodes, rejecting the rhetoric of white
supremacism in the memorable comment, 'We are not the same. I'm an
American. You're a sick asshole'. Nick responds by handcuffing D-Fens to
detain him while he calls the police so that they can arrest him. He goes
through the gym bag and, finding the unicorn snow globe, calls it 'faggot

Figure 8:   D-Fens and Nick reflected together, immediately before D-Fens shoots.

shit' and smashes it. Nick then effectively, as Richard Dyer (1997, p. 219) states, mounts D-Fens, taunting him that he will be 'fucked up the ass by some big buck nigger' in prison and repeating excitedly 'Give it to me, Give it to me'. As D-Fens falls to the floor, one of the lenses in his glasses is fractured. He manages to pull out the switchblade taken earlier from the gang members, and stabs Nick in the shoulder. D-Fens shoots him and then fires into a mirror reflecting images of the two of them (Figure 8).

Critics have argued that the primary intention behind the scene is to make sure that audiences do not see D-Fens as a right-wing bigot. The neo-Nazi 'secures a position we might otherwise be inclined to attribute to D-Fens' (Clover, 1993, p. 8). For Sharon Willis this is part of the deliberate strategy in *Falling Down* of obfuscating its actually deeply patriarchal and white-centred ideological orientation. She rightly points out that D-Fens's anger cannot so easily be distinguished from that of Nick, and several of John Gabriel's interviewees confirmed that film audiences read the reflection of D-Fens and Nick together in the mirror as suggesting that D-Fens had seen a hateful part of himself in Nick. It may be premature, though, to argue further that 'Nick...represents an exaggerated condensation of the tendencies that the film discourse wants to exploit' (Willis, 1997, p. 17). For Willis the film is ultimately anchored ideologically in the notion of 'home' as the seat of white patriarchal power, from which D-Fens is exiled but where Prendergast will finally reign (1997, p. 19). This scene only partially bears out this reading. It does begin to emphasise parallels in D-Fens's and Prendergast's dysfunctional home lives, in part through inserting two short scenes featuring Prendergast into the narrative during the time that D-Fens is in the surplus store. Again, it is home that D-Fens invokes as a last ditch attempt to avoid confrontation with Nick; 'I am not a vigilante. I am just trying to get home for my daughter's birthday'; but bearing out Willis's sense of the slippage between D-Fens and Nick, this slides into a threat, '...and if everybody leaves me alone no-one will get hurt'. However, the very beginning of the scene envisions the nuclear family in very different terms, which associate D-Fens's exile with a wider deficit in white masculinity.

Like several scenes in the film, including the ones with the black protester and those set in the Whammyburger, it starts with a high angle shot, in this case of telephone and electricity wires. As the camera pans down, it reveals a mural, past which D-Fens walks without noticing it.

The mural shows in part a man and a woman embracing, with a little girl on the woman's shoulders (Figure 9). He is black, she is Latina or possibly white, and gigantic butterflies complete the evocation of an idyllic heterosexual nuclear family. With the possible exception of the endangered family of the groundskeeper in the plastic surgeon's house, this is the only happy family depicted in the entire film. As such, even though the mural is on screen for a few seconds and probably does not attract much attention, it imagines the happy home in racial terms that preclude any of the film's white guys. Moreover as D-Fens reaches the side wall of what will be revealed as the surplus store this mural is supplanted by one much more in keeping with Nick's taste. Right next to the happy family image, four uniformed soldiers are depicted in combat poses, all of them white and male. The effect is to frame the entire surplus store scene via a racialised distinction between two contrasting masculinities; one white, militaristic, and all-male (which encompasses Nick and D-Fens); the other black,

Figure 9:   Outside the surplus store.

heterosexual, loving, and procreative (which remains peripheral, inscribed on the margins of the film).

The scene that ensues in the surplus store emphasises and eroticises this white hypermasculinity. Richard Dyer has observed how it 'binds together whiteness, homoeroticism, and violence', and his argument must be quoted in some detail:

> The two white gay men are customers, clearly looking for purchases charged with erotic violence ... After killing the store owner, D-Fens dresses up in the gear from the racks that the gay boys were going through and arms himself with the owner's bazooka. Thus, in both erotic tastes and actual action, gay men seem no less violent than the store owner, who in turn seems no less homosexual, while D-Fens is not so distant from this erotic culture of violence. There is a continuum between violence, asserted whiteness and homosexuality, and between D-Fens, the store owner, and the fag customers. (1997, p. 219)

Dyer explains the 'obsessive homosexual[ity]' of this sequence by reference to his notion of 'white death'; the idea that the normative discourse of whiteness as unmarked, universal, is haunted by a sense that its blankness is also a kind of deadness, a sterile, non-reproductive form of [in]humanity. Extrapolating from this, it could be argued the gay couple are not there to represent gay identity for itself; rather they are featured because of the prejudicial AIDS-era associations of homosexuality with sickness, death, and sterility. One of the major insights yielded by Dyer's general thesis is that these negative connotations of racial whiteness are inevitable results of the foundational definition of whiteness and its projection of particularity on to its other, blackness. It should theoretically be possible to disclose these negative connotations in all dominant constructions of white racial identity, given enough interpretative pressure. But the question remains as to the significance of why in this film, at this moment, the previously mutually reinforcing cohort of straight white masculinity is so spectacularly breaking apart.

What is clear is that the disturbance of identity goes further than is implied by the film's somewhat hackneyed relegation of Nick to the realms of political and sexual 'perversion' (so far as the latter is concerned, the implication is that Nick's sexism and racism are mixed up with, if not caused by, his repression of his own homosexuality). D-Fens and Nick are bound together not only by their status as white males, but also by their implicit search for some kind of authentic masculinity – a failed quest, as was signalled by the mural that D-Fens walks past without seeing it, and, in Nick's case, one that short-circuits into fascism. When Nick recommends the service-hardened Vietnam jungle boots rather than the new-fangled boots he also sells, which are 'scientifically engineered and all that crap' and consequently suitable only for 'pussies and faggots', he seems to be investing in an extreme, pathological form of the nostalgia that D-Fens evinced for '1965' when he was in Mr Lee's shop. But in rendering this search for authentic masculinity in such homophobic and pathological terms, the possibility of any kind of redemptive or 'natural' masculinity is foreclosed. Compounding this is the commercial function of the surplus store itself, which sells the trappings of masculinity and militarism to anyone – as exemplified by the gay couple, and another woman customer shown exiting the shop at the beginning of the scene – at the exact moment that such trappings have lost the ability to confer power. Nick's rage at this is evident in his harassment of the gay couple and his overt standing on his 'right' to serve only those clients he chooses. As for D-Fens, in the aftermath of his slaying of Nick, he is shown calling Beth again on the telephone, having donned an army jacket from the surplus store (Figure 10). Whilst the camera tracks slowly round the back room of the store, he tells her that, like astronauts on a malfunctioning craft who are still committed to orbit the moon, he has 'passed the point of no return'. While primarily signalling a decisive moment in D-Fens's descent into violence and in his harassment of Beth, the phase also indicates a loss of status. From now on the police will track him as the white guy 'dressed as GI Joe', the children's action figure.[16] As much as this scene presents D-Fens as falling victim to a 'perverse' homoeroticism, it may be that it signals commodification as the greater threat to white male autonomy.

Between Good Guys and Bad Guys

The climactic scene of the film culminates in a shootout on Venice Pier between the two white guys who have emerged as the key players.[17] Having taken the injured Sandra's gun, Prendergast finally catches up with D-Fens shortly after he has caught up with Beth and Adele. Clearly besotted with Adele and massively resentful towards Beth, D-Fens forces her to embrace him and reiterates a veiled death threat that he had made by telephone from the back room of the surplus store.

Though it is Beth who will effectively disarm D-Fens, as soon as Prendergast appears the scene is dominated by the relationship between the two men, the parallels and differences between them as paternal figures and as renegade *versus* agent of law and order. In what ways then, if at all, does the resolution of the film's narrative resolve the ideological 'crisis of white masculinity' embodied by both Prendergast and D-Fens throughout?

This closing 14 minutes or so on and around Venice Pier contain many of the most powerful scenes in the film: D-Fens's tenderness towards his daughter Adele, Beth kicking away D-Fens's gun, Prendergast's emergence and coolness under pressure, the shot D-Fens's slow motion fall

Figure 10: 'Sugar, does this ring a bell? Till death do us part?'

backwards over the railings into the ocean, Prendergast's paternal chat with Adele, and the final seconds showing the old video of Bill, Beth, Adele, and their Labrador puppy happily celebrating Adele's second birthday. Yet most of the major critics of the movie devote comparatively little space to discussing the climax of the film. For Sharon Willis, the scene seems worthy of little comment, as it directly enacts Prendergast's 'positioning as the "good guy"' which has already taken 'shape around his success in securing dominance over his crazed wife and in reclaiming his *home* through this patriarchal posturing' (1997, p. 18). Having finally put his own house in order both domestically and professionally, Prendergast protects Beth and Adele and ultimately extirpates D-Fens. In like fashion Liam Kennedy reads the emergence of Prendergast as revitalising the old American trope of 'redemption through violence' (Slotkin, 1992) by substituting for the lone white vigilante a more 'liberal' hero who takes responsibility for his own problems. Kennedy argues that the film might parody 'the imperial individualism of white American manhood', but it ultimately remakes it by appropriating the victim status associated with people of colour 'as a morality tale for a multiracial, postnational United States' that remains culturally centred on white masculinity (2000, p. 41). Paul Gormley makes a similar point by reference to *Falling Down*'s position with respect to 1990s American cinema. He argues that the film differentiates itself from the 'backlash' trajectory of Douglas's earlier works, typified by *Fatal Attraction*, and also from the direct audience identifications of the action movie. But it does so by appropriating the racial anger articulated in *Boyz N the Hood*, *Menace II Society*, and other films by African Americans (2005, pp. 58–60, 67), principally via the two young black males who respond to D-Fens in the Whammyburger restaurant and in connection with the rocket launcher. As Gormley sees it, *Falling Down*

> appropriates what it sees as the affective power of African American culture, but then dismisses such immediacy as primitive and childlike. *Falling Down* is an attempt to be 'smarter' than the new Black Realism,

> by breaking down the heroic status of its angry violent man, and
> turning him into a regressive psychotic. (2005, p. 68)

For all three of these critics then, in spite of the confusions and ambiguities
that characterise the film as a whole, the ending offers a coherent
ideological resolution, or a 'more monolithic viewing position' (2005, p. 68),
which has been predetermined by Prendergast's emergence as the nemesis
of D-Fens.

Richard Dyer devotes a little more attention to the ending, and he is
also more sensitive to *Falling Down*'s 'highly ambivalent' tone (1997, p. 220).
Willis, Kennedy, and Gormley seek to uncover the film's ideological project,
which they see as rejuvenating imperialist and patriarchal white masculinity
in a multicultural nation. Dyer is more concerned with the different versions
of whiteness that the film puts into play. He maps D-Fens and Prendergast
according to different kinds of white racial identity, ranging from extreme
to unmarked and normative, and couches his conclusion by reference to the
implications of privileging each of these. 'If *Falling Down* is Bill/Douglas's
film' Dyer argues, 'then it may be felt to articulate the idea that whiteness,
especially white masculinity, is under threat, decentred, angry, keying in to
an emergent discourse of the 1990s' (1997, p. 222) – what we might think of
as the discourse of the 'crisis of white masculinity' whose expansiveness was
charted in Parts 2 and 3 of this book. However, if 'it is Prendergast's [film]
it is resecuring the culturally stronger, but now harder to maintain position
of ordinariness, the subject without properties'. Dyer adds a third possibility,
suggested by the very last frames of the film, which close in on the old video
of the Foster-Travino family celebrating Adele's second birthday, before
abruptly cutting off sound and vision:

> ...if the final images have the last word, it is in line with the much
> deeper anxieties of the *Zombie* and *Alien* films and of *Blade Runner*, a
> feeling that deep down whites are nothing and have had their day, that
> we are, and perhaps always have been, the dead. (1997, p. 222)

This possible reading almost precisely inverts those of Willis and Kennedy. Where they see *Falling Down* as trying to rejuvenate white masculinity through Prendergast, Dyer sees it as revealing the inevitable but long-obscured contradictions of dominant Western ideologies of whiteness.

After the arguments made thus far, it will surprise few readers to insist again on the scene's ambiguity and its solicitation of mixed and shifting identifications. This is most striking at the level of character, where D-Fens's tenderness towards Adele and aggression towards Beth cannot help but leave audiences in some confusion.[18] In parallel, Prendergast's new status as the good guy is open to question. From the moment when Beth, at a signal from the cop, kicks away D-Fens's gun, and the two men bellow contradictory orders to her, to flee or to stay, Prendergast starts to take over the role of head of the Foster-Travino household. Having dispatched D-Fens and sworn at his boss Captain Yardley as the latter is being interviewed on live television, he seeks out Beth, who immediately submits to his authority, asking him what she should do about Adele's birthday. He then sits next to Adele on the steps outside her house and acts as what can only be described as a surrogate father, telling her that 'If I had a little girl, I would want her to be called Adele'. Surely there is a sense of usurpation here which can only be partially compensated by Prendergast's heroic defence of the females and by audiences' sympathy with him as a bereaved father.

The dialogue in this scene distinguishes between 'good guys' and 'bad guys', but the effect is more to problematise the imposition of such binary oppositions than to clarify these ambiguities. This terminology is introduced by Prendergast, when he tries to talk D-Fens down from Venice Pier, telling him 'Let's meet some nice policeman. They're good guys'. Such a characterisation of course flies in the face of Prendergast's experiences with his colleagues who have, with the exception of non-guy Sandra Torres, acted detestably throughout. D-Fens then recodes the distinction twice, first in the wondering, 'I'm the bad guy?', which signals to audiences a very 1990s sense of the victimisation of white masculinity, and then when he challenges Prendergast to a 'showdown between the sheriff and the bad guy', a framework that Prendergast eventually reluctantly accepts. There are echoes here both of the classical Western, and the partial domestication of the violent male protector figure in contemporary revisionist Westerns such as Clint Eastwood's 1992 *Unforgiven* (which, into the bargain, involves another white/black buddy relationship). However, much as audiences and critics have registered these references, the immediate context of the good guy/ bad guy distinction is strongly determined by Prendergast's status as a cop seeking to arrest D-Fens. Prendergast's line about the 'good guy' policemen invokes a sweeping binary opposition that, as social geographer Steve Herbert has shown, played an important role in organising perspectives on law and order in the territorialised space of Los Angeles. As Herbert puts it

> The term 'bad guy' is ubiquitous in police discourse ... The police, by contrast, represent the good whose mission it is to protect society from the predatory tendencies of evil criminals ... By labelling their opponents 'bad guys' police officers simultaneously represent themselves as virtuous agents of the good, willing to risk their lives to ensure peace to the citizenry. These moral distinctions extend to geographical areas as well: immoral areas are referred to as 'dirty' and thus in need of the cleansing of police territorial action. In these areas, which are likely to be heavily populated by minorities, officers believe that violence is an inherent part of life, and thus that it must be met with violence. (1996, p. 577)

Herbert's argument was apparently borne out by incidents such as the beating of Rodney King, if conspicuously not by the LAPD's failure to control the outbreak of urban violence in April–May 1992. It is this vigilante logic also that was highlighted and legally tested in the cases of Bernhard Goetz and Soon Ja Du/Latasha Harlins. In *Falling Down* it has already been apparent in the doubly territorialised perspective from which Detectives Jones and Sanchez, backed up by Captain Yardley, had warned Prendergast off 'their' case, in the belief that a white guy in south Central

Figure 11: 'A showdown between the sheriff and the bad guy'.

Los Angeles could not be the source of criminality. In a way, Prendergast's earlier refusal to leave his desk represents a refusal to adopt this territorialised logic, one that chimes with his compassionate outlook and the suggestion that he is intended to represent liberal values. So his use of the good guy/bad guy discourse here represents the surrendering of his previously liberal stance and the adoption of his colleagues' territorialised logic of criminality. He employs this logic effectively to reverse their earlier assumption, interpolating D-Fens as *wholly bad*. In the good guy/bad guy discourse, it is not possible to be fatally flawed or ambivalent, so Prendergast claims that he 'knows' that D-Fens intends to kill his wife and child, while D-Fens is in fact tender and caring towards child after child throughout the movie, and the editing emphasises that he puts his gun down each time he starts talking to Adele, the second time inadvertently allowing himself to be disarmed. And finally, it is this discourse that leads Prendergast to mis-recognise D-Fens's threat and to shoot him, allowing D-Fens to engineer his own death as a kind of self-sacrifice so that, in his mind at least, his daughter will inherit insurance money (Figure 11).

Visually, during the shootout Prendergast is flanked by evidence of the permeability of distinctions between good guy and bad guy. The advertising posters for the hiphop star Hammer clearly visible behind Prendergast suggest a much wider and more culturally sophisticated sense of space, 'race', and masculinity. Hammer, whose naked torso is prominently displayed here, is generally regarded as the first hiphop performer to achieve mainstream success. During the period that *Falling Down* was being made and released he was in fact reinventing his star persona so as to appear 'harder', in line with the increasing importance of figurations of gang violence in defining hiphop authenticity (this in part entailed the temporary dropping of 'M.C.' from his stage name). Aside from the apparent ease with which Hammer could deploy the pose of the 'bad guy', as an icon of masculinity it would be hard to conceive of a more powerful combination of performing and composing talent, fame, entrepreneurial success, and business acumen – one that has continued into the present.

How to make sense of all this? It should be clear that the point is not at all to validate D-Fens, whose assault on Beth in this scene spills over from verbal to physical, and creates a real fear for her life. At the same time, the good guy/bad guy discourse is fatally undermined, leaving audiences without a framework to negotiate the mixed and conflicting appeals of D-Fens and Prendergast. Now it is certainly possible to read all this along the lines suggested by Kennedy and Gormley, in terms of the appropriation of tropes of black identity in order to substantiate a rationale of white male victimisation. However, the visual presence of the hiphop star Hammer in the backdrop to the showdown between Prendergast and D-Fens opens a new dimension. The identification of Hammer's combined star persona, wealth, fame, and masculine performance within blackness provides an economically and culturally successful counterpart to the 'not economically viable' man. If a racial ideology is at work here, it would seem to be identifying whiteness with exclusion and lack, rather than re-securing its privileges.

The posters of Hammer are only the last of a series of positively charged representations of blackness inhabiting the *margins* of the film: the various black boys and adolescents; the protester outside the bank; the romanticised black 'husband' figure in the street mural. It is hard to quantify the extent to which these images of black masculinity register on audiences.

Although they originate as counterpoints to the deficit status of D-Fens's whiteness, their cumulative effect spills over beyond merely signalling the obsolescence of traditional forms of white masculinity, to its displacement by more culturally dynamic black forms. It may well be that their distancing from the film's primary diegesis, rather than marginalising them as might be expected, signals an ability to resist the crisis affecting the white guys. This is one reason the black feminist critic bell hooks has suggested that '[t]here is a way to talk about *Falling Down* as describing the end of Western civilization'. hooks launches an optimistic reading of the film as working through white males' blaming of others for the fact that 'white supremacist patriarchy isn't working for white people' (1994, p. 50), to suggest the necessity of an oppositional understanding of crisis that goes beyond a narrow identity politics. For hooks, there is a utopian possibility here that is foreclosed in certain contemporary films claiming to represent black culture (*Menace II Society* in particular). As she points out, 'in *Falling Down* the white man is not still standing. He hasn't conquered the turf. There's this whole sense of, "Yeah, you now see what everyone else has been seeing, which is that the planet has been fucked up and you're going to be a victim of it too"' (1994, p. 52).

These speculations implicitly contest the sense of *Falling Down*'s parasitism upon black culture (as in Kennedy, 2000; Gormley, 2005), and suggest a rethinking of the film's depiction of a territorialised Los Angeles dominated by different groups intent on protecting their territory. In the popular controversy and in much academic criticism, this has been interpreted negatively, either as a nightmare vision of multiculturalism, shorthand for a nation divided into special interest groups, and/or one suffering for its lack of traditional (patriarchal, white) values. Such readings position *Falling Down* as a rejection of and withdrawal from multiculturalism. Yet the ending's lack of resolution may also point towards the need, not to abandon that project, but to perfect it.

✖ P<small>ART</small> 5

THE LEGACY OF *FALLING DOWN*

Debate Movies and Film Theory

In February 2007 journalists Mark Townsend and David Smith announced in the London *Observer* that 'Almost fifteen years after Michael Douglas played an ordinary man betrayed by society, Britain has its own *Falling Down*' (Townsend and Smith, 2007). They were referring to *Outlaw*, Nick Love's film about a returning Iraq war veteran (Sean Bean) who leads a group of vigilantes. Nevertheless, *Falling Down* has generally been seen as too much of an 'unconventional thriller', as the blurb on the 2000 DVD release put it, to serve as much of a blueprint for other films. The only film for which it has served as a major reference point is Bobcat Goldthwaite's *God Bless America* (2012), a satirical thriller in which a middle-aged white male (Joel Murray) and a 16-year-old white girl (Tara Lynne Barr) go on a killing spree that culminates on the set of a television talent show that is a parodic version of 'American Idol'. *God Bless America* was generally received as a potentially interesting film let down by a lack of clarity over the object of its satire – essentially, the stupidity of American consumers, or the culture that caters to a perception of that stupidity – and weak execution, especially its pacing. While some praised *God Bless America* for its 'irreverent and bold social satire' (Munro 2012), most saw it as 'militant and muddled' (Shaffer, 2012), if not utterly wrongheaded. The critical consensus on this '*Falling Down* for the internet and media generation' (Pulaski, 2012), was sadly, 'not so much *Falling Down* as falling flat' (Solomons, 2012).

While these negative critical reviews parallel certain aspects of the popular controversy over *Falling Down*, there are few signs that *God Bless America* was able to turn ideological ambiguity to such productive ends. The various controversies charted in this book suggest, if nothing else, the difficulty of identifying *Falling Down* with a specific ideological position. But by now it should be clear that the essential incoherence of *Falling Down* is not only part of its significance, but has also helped to define its position in cinema history. The film typified the 1990s phenomenon of 'talkies': films that engaged controversial topics and set out to pro-

Figure 12:   Michael Douglas and Demi Moore in the 'talkie' *Disclosure*.

voke discussion among audiences. Such films, in many of which Michael
Douglas was involved, deliberately catered to viewers who might affiliate
with a variety of characters, qualities, and debating positions. Hence the
'battle of the sexes' themes of *Fatal Attraction* and *The War of the Roses*
invited polarised investments from male and female viewers, which were
incorporated into their marketing as date movies sparking discussion over
issues such as sexual fidelity and divorce. Other talkies contemporaneous
with *Falling Down* similarly testified to the penetration of feminism, civil
rights activism, and gay activism into mainstream American culture – or,
as some would argue, were the means by which Hollywood co-opted
identity politics. Spike Lee's revision of the classical Hollywood biopic in
Malcolm X was, like *Falling Down*, funded by Warner Bros, albeit with a
budget that Lee regarded as inadequate (see Lee with Wiley, 1993, pp. 23,
31–32, 122–123, 165–166). Another talkie, *Philadelphia* (1993), was from
the first conceptualised as a film that played to audiences ranging from
gay-identified to homophobic. 'We felt we would fail if our movie played
to people who already…believe that people shouldn't discriminate against
homosexuals', argued *Philadelphia* screenwriter Ron Nyswaner, 'If our

movie only played to people who thought just like we do, we would have done nothing very significant' (Epstein and Friedman, 1995).

A crucial point here is that when Hollywood and identity politics collided in the late 1980s and early 1990s, this put at stake not only traditional racial and gendered hierarchies but also notions of film form that depend upon decoding a unitary ideological meaning or defining a single preferred viewing position. *Falling Down* looks down this telescope from both ends. In its tendency to universalise the position of the embattled white males Prendergast and D-Fens, and in its depiction of gendered, ethnic, and class stereotypes such as Prendergast's nagging wife, the Korean storekeeper, the Latino gang members, and the homeless man, it reinforces the traditional biases of dominant American culture. Yet in defamiliarising the figure of the white male father, and in laying bare the pathological aspects of dominant forms of white racial identity, the film marks a pivotal moment in the trajectory of identity representation in American cinema.

This moment has had an impact on academic approaches to film. It is noticeable that around the mid-1990s the older forms of identity criticism focusing on stereotyping and positive or negative images gave way to work like that discussed in Part 4, that investigated, on the one hand, the more strategic 'uses' of identity formations and, on the other, the diversity of viewers' pleasures and interpretations. At the same time, rather than organising critical approaches on the basis of one form of identity, typically gender or 'race', critics saw the necessity to explore the ways in which different forms of identity intercut, overlapped, or were contrasted. Sub-titles such as Elizabeth Traube's 'Class, Gender and Generation in 1980s film', and Sharon Willis's 'Race and Gender in Contemporary Hollywood Film' testified to this shift. More recently, work such as Donna Peberdy's (2011) on performances of 'male angst' both on and off the film screen has returned to more identity-specific themes but with a renewed, avowedly pluralist critical apparatus.

The High-Water Mark of White Male Paranoia

Michael Douglas's next film, the Barry Levinson-directed *Disclosure* (1994), marked the peak of the 'white male in crisis' theme in Hollywood (Figure 12). With its tagline 'Sex Is Power', the film was overtly marketed as a thriller about workplace sexual harassment, with the twist that, unlike the vast majority of such cases in actuality, the aggressor was female (Meredith Johnson, played by Demi Moore) and the victim, accused of being the harasser, male (Douglas as Tom Sanders).

As a backlash movie against challenges to the white family man, *Disclosure* is both ideologically simpler and more obviously conservative, as well as being more coherent than *Falling Down*. In the latter Rachel Ticotin's role as Sandra Torres explicitly contests the boorishness of colleagues such as Lydecker, and partially ameliorates Captain Yardley's machismo. Moore, as Johnson, seems much closer to the traditional Hollywood *femme fatale* whose entry into the workplace is portrayed as disrupting the patriarchal order. 'My God! She's in the system', exclaims Sanders at one point as he encounters Johnson's avatar while trying to rescue computer files. Back in the domestic sphere, Douglas gives vent to white male victimhood much more explicitly than he had done in *Falling Down*. When his wife, career lawyer Susan (Caroline Goodall), suggests that he responds to the charge of sexual harassment by apologising to save his job, Sanders explodes 'Why don't I just admit it? Why don't I just be that guy, that evil white male that you're all complaining about? I liked that; then I could fuck anybody'. He calls the family's (Asian) maid downstairs mockingly to exercise this 'patriarchal urge' before rounding on Susan with the understanding of sexual harassment he has just acquired from his legal adviser. 'Sexual harassment is about power, not sex. When did I have the power?' These lines represent the high-water mark of the crisis of, or paranoia about, white masculinity in Hollywood.

Disclosure itself goes on to undercut the importance of sexual politics. The sexual harassment narrative which was used to sell the film is resolved a full 27 minutes before the end. In that final quarter it transpires that the whole issue has been a smokescreen, a device deployed by the top brass of Sanders's company to sideline him until the company is taken over by another. Sanders's revelations about cost-cutting at a Malaysian production facility could have torpedoed the merger that not only stands to make a great deal of money for Digicom's owners, but also precludes this American tech company being taken over by foreign capital. So the narrative of sexual harassment and the white male in crisis turns out to be overdetermined by global capitalism and the emergence of Pacific Rim economies.

Marketing for Changing Times

As the furore over the 'crisis of white masculinity' has dissipated, the marketing of *Falling Down* to consumers has downplayed its relationship to popular controversy and emphasised instead its place in the thriller/action movie genre. Both the initial release on video cassette (1993) and its subsequent one on DVD (2000) prominently featured the artwork of the original film poster. Their front covers are dominated by a full-length image of Douglas on the hill in gangland, with the skyscrapers of Los Angeles in the background. He carries a briefcase in one hand and (out of synch with the film's narrative sequence) a shotgun in the other. The image fills all the available space, without any borders, and lettering is set into it. Both of the film's sub-titles are given: 'A Tale of Urban Reality' and 'The adventures of an ordinary man at war with the everyday world' (revised for the DVD release to 'The adventure of an ordinary man at war with the everyday world'). The blurb on the back cover of the DVD emphasises the latter, before slipping into Charles Bronson thriller mode: 'Freeways are clogged. Terror stalks our cities. At shops and restaurants, the customer is seldom right. The pressures of big city life can anger anyone. But Bill Foster is more than angry. He's out to get even'. The blurb ends by quoting a headline from one of the March 1993 *Los Angeles Times* articles on the film (Rauzi, 1993). '*Falling Down* is … a spellbinding, unconventional thriller that asks, "Are we falling apart?"'[19]

This prioritisation of topical crisis over thriller is reversed in the packaging design of the 2009 DVD and Blu-ray release, which dispenses with the original cover image and taglines, adapting a close-up of Douglas's face which had been on the back cover. It is heavily cropped and framed by borders and text. This image trades on Douglas's star persona, and possibly references a publicity shot of Dustin Hoffman for *Straw Dogs*, implicitly assimilating the 'crisis' into the longer historical sweep of the 'melodrama of beset masculinity' discussed in Part 3 earlier.

The End of Men, or White Male Paranoia Redux

Hollywood's discourses of gender and 'race' have changed greatly since 1993, so much so that the protests and the anger over *Falling Down*'s representations of racial, ethnic, and gendered identity seem to belong to a different age; voices in an argument which has been resolved, largely in progressive terms. Yet the post 9/11 invisibility of white masculinity as a problematic is, arguably, just as remarkable a cultural phenomenon as the exaggerated visibility associated with the moment of 'crisis' emblematised by *Falling Down*. The 1990s social and economic problematic described by Susan Faludi seems, if anything, to have become worse, as a largely post-industrial workplace increasingly distances itself from values that have remained stubbornly attached to white masculinity. As Hanna Rosin points out in 2012's *The End of Men: And the Rise of Women*, updating the arguments of Faludi's *Stiffed*, three-quarters of the 7.5 million jobs in the post 2008 recession were lost by men, but this only accelerated a gendered shift that had been going on for 30 years or more. Since 2009, according to Rosin, for the first time in American history, there were more women than men in the American workforce (the United Kingdom reached the same point around a year later). At the same time, the prestige of masculinity has fallen, and 'our vast and struggling middle class, where the disparities between men and women are the greatest, is slowly turning into a matriarchy, with men increasingly absent from the workforce and from home, as women make all the decisions' (Rosin, 2012, pp. 8, 10). This describes pretty neatly the gendered world inhabited by D-Fens. His story articulates a social and economic problematic of masculinity that, for all the efforts of critics such as Faludi and Rosin, has been forgotten or obscured to a greater extent than it has been resolved.

With regard to white masculinity, *Falling Down* makes visible a controversy that over the last two decades seems to be continually erased and occasionally made visible again, while for those at the economic sharp end it has never gone away. The film's depiction of femininity and of racial and ethnic difference much more clearly addresses contemporary areas of controversy. Here the film resonates directly with the rightward ideological trajectory of the Republican Party in America. The 'culture wars' agenda articulated by Patrick Buchanan at the Republican Party Convention while *Falling Down* was in post-production represented a minority view in the party in September 1992. Many of its central planks, such as opposition to abortion and gay marriage, have since become mainstream Republican policy. Yet much about *Falling Down* evades or exceeds these controversies, in particular its marginalised but fascinating depiction of African Americans.

A final legacy of *Falling Down* might be seen in the longer, serial format of television series such as *The Sopranos* (1999–2007), *The Wire* (2002–2008), and *Breaking Bad* (2008–2013). *The Sopranos* and *Breaking Bad* especially have picked up where *Falling Down* left off, depicting family-orientated men whose profoundly alienating qualities are gradually revealed. As critic Emily Nussbaum has put it, the difference is that between the 'antihero drama, in which we root for a bad boy in spite of ourselves', and a much more ambivalent viewing experience of television such as the late seasons of *The Sopranos* and *Breaking Bad* that dare 'to punish its audience for loving a monster' (2012, p. 82). In comparison, D-Fens has come to seem fairly tame.

✖ APPENDICES

Appendix A: Key Details

Cast

D-Fens	Michael Douglas	Seedy Guy in Park	John Fleck
Prendergast	Robert Duvall	Rick (Whammyburger)	Brent Hinkley
Beth	Barbara Hershey	Sheila (Whammyburger)	Dedee Pfeiffer
Sandra	Rachel Ticotin	Woman Who Throws Up	
Mrs Prendergast	Tuesday Weld	(Whammyburger)	Carol Androsky
Surplus Store Owner	Frederic Forrest	Lita the Waitress	Margaret Medina
D-Fens' Mother	Lois Smith	Not Economically	
Adele (Beth's child)	Joey Hope Singer	Viable Man	Vondie Curtis-Hall
Guy on Freeway	Ebbe Roe Smith	Annoying Man at Phone	
Mr Lee	Michael Paul Chan	Booth	Mark Frank
Captain Yardley	Raymond J. Barry	First Gay Man	Peter Radon
Detective Lydecker	D.W. Moffet	Second Gay Man	Spencer Rochfort
Detective Brian	Steve Park	Second Office at Beth's	Carole Ita White
Detective Jones	Kimberly Scott	Second Officer's Partner	Russell Curry
Detective Keene	James Keane	Guy Behind Woman Driver	John Fink
Detective Graham	Macon McCalman	Street Worker	Jack Kehoe
Detective Sanchez	Richard Montoya	Kid (with Missile Launcher)	Valentino D.
Police Clerk	Bruce Beatty		Harrison
Officer at Station	Mathew Saks	Frank (Golfer)	Jack Betts
Gang Member One	Agustin Rodriguez	Jim (Golfer)	Al Mancini
Gang Member Two	Eddie Frias	Dad (Back Yard Party)	John Diehl
Gang Member Three	Pat Romano	Mom (Back Yard Party)	Amy Morton
Gang Member Four	Fabio Urena	Trina (Back Yard Party)	Abbey Barthel
Angie	Karina Arroyave	Suzie the Stripper	Susie Singer
Angie's Mother	Irene Olga Lopez	Paramedic	Wayne Duvall
Uniformed Officer at Beth's	Benjamin Mouton	Prendergast's daughter	Valisha Jean Malin
Uniformed Officer's Partner	Dean Hallo	CHP Officer Bobbit	Jeffrey Byron
Construction Sign Man			(uncredited)
by Bus Stop	James Morrison		

Production Crew

Director	Joel Schumacher			Howard
Producers	Arnold Kopelson	Co-Producers		Dan Kolsrud
	Herschel Weingrod	Stephen Brown		
	Timothy Harris			Nana Greenwald
Written by	Ebbe Roe Smith	Associate Producers		William S. Beasley
Director of Photography	Andrzej Bartkowiak			Ebbe Roe Smith
Production Designer	Barbara Ling			John J. Tomko
Editor	Paul Hirsch	Casting by		Marion Dougherty
Music by	James Newton	Art Direction by		Larry Fulton

Other Details

Released
26 February 1993 (US), 4 June 1993 (UK).
Budget
$25–30 million.
Opening Weekend: $8, 724, 452.
Gross: $40, 903, 593 (US).

Certification and Ratings

Argentina: 16
Australia: M
Brazil: 16
Canada: 18A
Finland: 16
France: 12
Germany: 16
Iceland: 16
Italy: VM14
Netherlands: 12
Philippines: R18
Portugal: M16
Singapore: NC16
South Korea: 18
Spain: 18
Sweden: 15
UK: 18
USA: R (for violence and strong language)

Appendix B: Notes

1 Though offered somewhat in the playful spirit of its ultimate source in Shakespeare's *Twelfth Night,* this taxonomy usefully differentiates between the deliberate provocations made by movies such as *Fahrenheit 9/11*; struggles over films such as *The Birth of a Nation*, which has been contested by African American critics and film-makers since its release; and examples like *A Clockwork Orange*, which was largely rendered controversial by alleged 'copycat' crimes, on which see Krämer, 2011.

2 Throughout this book the term 'race' is placed in inverted commas, in order to acknowledge its social and cultural currency while emphasising its lack of biological justification. I also wish to signal here the importance of what Cornel West termed in a highly influential 1990 essay 'the profoundly hybrid character of what we mean by "race", "ethnicity", and "nationality"'. As West explains, 'European immigrants arrived on American shores perceiving themselves as "Irish", "Sicilian", "Lithuanian", and so on. They had to learn that they were "white" principally by adopting an American discourse of positively valued whiteness and negatively charged blackness' (1999, p. 131). *Falling Down*, as will be argued in Part 4 of this book, signals the partial unravelling of this historical process. Until then, for simplicity's sake, the conceptual complex around 'race', ethnicity, and national identity identified by West is condensed into the single term 'race'.

3 Smith gives a detailed account of the composition and revision of his screenplay in an undated (c. 2012) interview available at the very useful fan site http://fallingdownfilm.com/ (accessed 21 September 2012). Some of the same points are made with less detail in his comments on the 2009 DVD release of *Falling Down*.

4 Unless noted, excerpts from reviews are taken from metacritic.com; http://www.metacritic.com/movie/falling-down.

5 All starring Charles Bronson as a peaceful architect turned vigilante, four *Death Wish* films had appeared by 1987, the first three of which were directed by Michael Winner. A final film, *Death Wish V* was released after *Falling Down*, in 1994. Their settings alternate between New York and Los Angeles. Reviews of *Falling Down* generally refer to *Death Wish*, though by 1993 this could easily be taken as referring to the series of films as a whole.

6 Interestingly, Canby compares *Falling Down* with John Cheever's *New Yorker* short story 'The Swimmer', upon which the 1968 movie was based (Canby 1993).

7 These questions would be addressed further in various attempts to gauge exactly how different audiences responded to the film, notably by the *Los Angeles Times* (see below) and in academic criticism (see Part 3).

8 Park's argument is discussed in more detail alongside the analysis of this scene in Part 4.

9 The same ambiguity is present in a slightly different version of Schumacher's remarks reported in the British film magazine *Empire*: 'There have been several movies in the US about anger in the street, but they had all been by African Americans. Well, they're not the only angry people in the United States' (Salisbury, 1993, p. 77).

10 Schumacher retells the Bening anecdote with slight variations in the commentary track on the 2009 Blu-ray edition of the film: 'She walked out, into New York, into the street at about two o'clock in the afternoon, and she said that she had three very distinct fears that travelled with her down the street. First, she thought, "What kind of a world am I bringing my child up in?" Then she started noticing the men on the street that she was passing, and she thought, "Any one of these people could be like the character that Michael Douglas plays [in our film]"; and by the time she reached Sixth Avenue, she said that her worst fear was, that she knows somewhere inside her that maybe she could become a person like Michael Douglas was in the movie.'

11 For a detailed exposition of how these insights from critical race studies were developed in film criticism, see Davies and Smith, 1997, pp. 50–69.

12 Several critics and reviewers have noted the similarity of the opening scene to the dream sequence at the beginning of Federico Fellini's *8½* (1963). Fellini's film also opens in a traffic jam, centres on a male alone in his car, and shows a variety of people in neighbouring cars gazing intrusively at him; several shots are copied almost exactly in *Falling Down.* A major difference lies in the very mixed ethnic and racial make-up of the people in surrounding cars. Overall there is comparatively little evidence that the comparison has shaped audiences' readings of the scene.

13 For an alternative reading of this scene focusing on the can of 'classic' coca cola as a deteriorated symbol of American power and cultural harmony, see Davies 1995a, pp. 229–231.

14 Richard Dyer explores these associations further in the closing section of *White*, entitled 'White Death' (Dyer, 1997, pp. 217–223), discussed in the 'Between Good Guys and Bad Guys' section later.

15 See Gormley, *The New Brutality Film*, pp. 43–71, for an alternative reading of the film, grounded in very different understandings of mis-recognition in general and the black protester in particular, whom Gormley reads as 'a pitiful figure' (p. 60) whose failure to understand his own situation parallels that of D-Fens.

16 For British readers, the approximate equivalent of GI Joe is Action Man.

17 Please see the synopsis section of this book for a detailed summary of the scene.

18 Compare Krin Gabbard's passing comment that 'Of the many films in which white males face challenges from blacks, women, immigrants, and other previously disempowered groups, *Falling Down...* is most often mentioned by critics. But this film problematises the confusion of D-Fens... The audience is invited to appreciate the irony in his final remark "*I'm* the bad guy?"' (Gabbard, 2001, p. 19). It is the complicated implications of this irony that have made the film so troublesome, or, rather, so interesting.

19 The blurb on the back of the original video cassette release is much more directly descriptive of the film, and aside from calling it a 'highly controversial and powerful new thriller' makes no reference to the popular controversy.

Appendix C: References

D'Addiero, Mercedes (1993) 'Does D-FENS Shatter American Reality or Reflect It? Grappling with a Lie That Tells the Truth', *Los Angeles Times*, 22 March, accessed online 29 July 2012 at http://articles.latimes.com/1993–03–22/entertainment/ca-13888_1_ times-film-critic.

Ansen, David (1993) 'Revenge of a Supernerd', *Newsweek*, 1 March, p. 80.

Appelo, Tim (1993) '"Down" Beat', *Entertainment Weekly*, 12 March, accessed online 30 July 2012 at http://www.ew.com/ew/article/0,,305859,00.html.

Baker, Bob (1993) 'The Urban Reality: Why (Heart) LA?' *Los Angeles Times* 15 March, accessed online 10 August 2012 at http://articles.latimes.com/1993–03–15/entertainment/ca-387_1_los-angeles.

Barkin, Steve M. (2003) *American Television News: The Media Marketplace and the Public Interest.* Armonk, NY: M. E. Sharpe, Inc.

Barlowe, Jamie (1994) 'The Always Already Crisis of Male Subjectivity or, the Penultimate "Melodramas of Beset [American(ist)] Manhood"', *Novel: A Forum on Fiction* 27:3, pp. 305–308.

Baym, Nina (1981) 'Melodramas of Beset Manhood: How Theories of American Fiction Exclude Women Authors', *American Quarterly* 33:2, pp. 123–139.

Bergesen, Albert and Max Herman (1998) 'Immigration, Race and Riot: The 1992 Los Angeles Uprising', *American Sociological Review* 63:1 (February), pp. 39–54.

Brown, Heloise (1999) 'Introduction', in Brown, Gilkes, and Kaloski-Naylor, *White?Women: Critical Perspectives on Race and Gender.* York: Raw Nerve Press, pp. 1–22.

Brown, Stephanie, and Keith Clark (2003) 'Melodramas of Beset Black Manhood?: Meditations on African American Masculinity as Scholarly Topos and Social Menace. An Introduction', *Callaloo* 26:3, pp. 732–737.

Buchanan, Patrick J. (1992a) 'Speech to National Republican Party Convention', 17 August, transcription by Michael E. Eidenmuller, accessed online 8 October 2012 at http://www.scribd.com/doc/70249364/Patrick-Buchanan-1992-RNC-culture-war.

Buchanan, Patrick J. (1992b) '1992 RNC Culture War', accessed online 8 October 2012 at http://www.scribd.com/doc/70249364/Patrick-Buchanan-1992-RNC-culture-war.

Callinicos, Alex (1992) 'Meaning of Los Angeles Riots', *Economic and Political Weekly* 25 July, pp. 1603–1606.

Canby, Vincent (1993) 'Review/Film; Urban Horrors, All Too Familiar', *New York Times* 16 February, accessed online 10 October 2012 at http://movies.nytimes.com/movie/review?res=9F0CE0DC113FF935A15751C0A965958260.

Chapman, Rowena and Jonathan Rutherford (1988) *Male Order: Unwrapping Masculinity.* London: Lawrence & Wishart.

Clover, Carol (1993) 'White Noise', *Sight and Sound*, May, pp. 6–9.

Cohan, Stephen and Ina Rae Hark, eds (1993) *Screening the Male: Exploring Masculinities in Hollywood Cinema*. London and New York: Routledge.

Collins, Jim, Hilary Radner, and Ava Preacher Collins (1993) *Film Theory Goes to the Movies.* London and New York: Routledge.

Corliss, Richard (1993) Review of *Falling Down*, *Time,* 1 March, p. 63.

Davies, Jude (1995a) 'Gender, Ethnicity and Cultural Crisis in *Falling Down* and *Groundhog Day*', *Screen* 25:3, pp. 214–232.

Davies, Jude (1995b) '"I'm the Bad Guy?" *Falling Down* and White Masculinity in 1990s Hollywood', *Journal of Gender Studies* 4:2, pp. 145–152.

Davies, Jude and Carol Smith (1997) *Gender, Ethnicity and Sexuality in Contemporary American Film*. Edinburgh: Edinburgh University Press.

Delgado, Richard and Jean Stefancic (1997) *Critical White Studies: Behind the Mirror.* Philadelphia: Temple University Press.

Dougan, Andy (2001) *Michael Douglas: Out of the Shadows: The Unauthorised Biography.* London: Robson Books.

Douglas, Kirk (1993) 'Does D-FENS Shatter American Reality or Reflect It?: My Son Is The Villain, Not The Hero, Of Urban Drama', *Los Angeles Times*, 22 March, accessed online 27 August 2012 at http://articles.latimes.com/1993–03–22/entertainment/ca-13887_1_los-angeles-times.

Douglas, Michael (2009) 'Deconstructing D-Fens: A Conversation with Michael Douglas', in Schumacher, 1993/2009.

Dyer, Richard (1988) 'White', *Screen* 28:4, pp. 44–64.

Dyer, Richard (1997) *White: Essays on Race and Culture.* London: Routledge.

Epstein, Rob and Jeffrey Friedman (1995) *The Celluloid Closet.*

Faludi, Susan (1991/1993) *Backlash: The Undeclared War Against [American] Women.* London: Vintage.

Faludi, Susan (1999) *Stiffed: The Betrayal of the Modern Man.* London: Chatto & Windus.

Fanon, Frantz (1952/1986) *Black Skin, White Masks.* London: Pluto.

Frankenberg, Ruth (1993) *White Women, Race Matters: The Social Construction of Whiteness.* Minneapolis: University of Minnesota Press.

Frankenberg, Ruth, ed (1995) *Displacing Whiteness: Essays in Social and Cultural Criticism.* Durham: Duke University Press.

Gabbard, Krin (2001) '"Someone Is Going to Pay": Resurgent White Masculinity in *Ransom*', in Peter Lehman, ed., *Masculinity: Bodies, Movies, Culture.* New York and London: Routledge/AFI Film Readers, pp. 7–23.

Gabriel, John (1996) 'What Do You Do when Minority Means You? *Falling Down* and the Construction of "Whiteness"', *Screen* 37:2, pp. 129–151.

Gates, David (1993) 'White Male Paranoia: Are They the New Victims or Just Bad Sports?' *Newsweek,* 28 March, pp. 48–53, accessed online 14 October 2012 at http://www.thedailybeast.com/newsweek/1993/03/29/white-male-paranoia.html.

Gooding-Williams, Robert, ed. (1993) *Reading Rodney King, Reading Urban Uprising.* New York and London: Routledge.

Gormley, Paul (2005) *The New-Brutality Film: Race and Affect in Contemporary Hollywood Cinema.* Bristol: Intellect.

Guerrero, Ed (1993) *Framing Blackness: The African American Image in Film.* Philadelphia: Temple University Press.

Hall, Stewart (1987) 'Minimal Selves', in *The Real Me: Post-Modernism and the Question of Identity.* London: ICA.

Hall, Stewart (1991) 'Old and New Identities: Old and New Ethnicities', in Anthony King, ed., *Culture, Globalization and the World System.* Basingstoke: Macmillan.

Herbert, Steve (1996) 'The Normative Ordering of Police Territoriality: Making and Marking Space with the Los Angeles Police Department', *Annals of the Association of American Geographers* 86:3 (September), pp. 567–582.

Hinson, Hal (1993) 'Falling Down', *Washington Post*, 26 February, accessed online 6 September 2012 at http://www.washingtonpost.com/wp-srv/style/longterm/movies/videos/fallingdownrhinson_a0a7f7.htm.

hooks, bell (1994) 'What's Passion Got To Do With It?' An interview with Marie-France Alderman, in *Outlaw Culture: Resisting Representations*, pp. 43–60. New York and Abingdon: Routledge.

Ignatiev, Noel and John Garvey, eds (1996) *Race Traitor.* New York and London: Routledge.

Jeffords, Susan (1989) *The Remasculinisation of America: Gender and the Vietnam War.* Bloomington: Indiana University Press.

Jeffords, Susan (1993) 'The Big Switch: Hollywood Masculinity in the Nineties', in Collins et al. *Film Theory Goes to the Movies*, pp. 196–208.

Jeffords, Susan (1994) *Hard Bodies: Hollywood Masculinity in the Reagan Era.* New Brunswick: Rutgers University Press.

Kennedy, Liam (1996) 'Alien Nation: White Male Paranoia and Imperial Culture in the United States', *Journal of American Studies* 30:1, pp. 87–100.

Kennedy, Liam (2000) *Race and Urban Space in Contemporary American Culture.* Edinburgh: Edinburgh University Press.

King, Peter H. (1993) 'A Walk Across the City', *Los Angeles Times*, 7 March, accessed online 27 August 2012 at http://articles.latimes.com/1993–03–07/news/mn-8334_1_los-angeles.

Kirkham, Pat and Janet Thumim eds (1993) *You Tarzan: Masculinity, Movies and Men*. London: Lawrence & Wishart.

Kirkham, Pat and Janet Thumim eds (1995) *Me Jane: Masculinity, Movies and Women*. London: Lawrence & Wishart.

Krämer, Peter (2011) *A Clockwork Orange*. Basingstoke: Palgrave Macmillan.

Lee, Spike with Ralph Wiley (1993) *By Any Means Necessary: The Trials and Tribulations of the Making of* Malcolm X. London: Vintage.

Linder, Doug (2011) 'The Trial of Bernhard Goetz', online at http://law2.umkc.edu/faculty/projects/ftrials/goetz/goetzaccount.html, accessed 23 October 2012.

Mathews, Jack (1993) 'La-La Land No More: Hollywood Used To Cast L.A. As a Shallow Place in the Sun But in Recent Films, It Plays the City of Diversity and Division', *Los Angeles Times,* 21 February, accessed online 29 July 2012 at http://articles.latimes.com/1993–02–21/entertainment/ca-939_1_los-angeles-image.

McBrier, Debra Branch, and George Wilson (2004) 'Going Down? Race and Downward Occupational Mobility for White-Collar Workers in the 1990s', *Work and Occupations*, 31:3, pp. 283–322.

Modleski, Tania (1991) *Feminism Without Women: Culture and Criticism in a 'Post-Feminist' Age*. New York and London: Routledge.

Morrison, Toni (1992) *Playing in the Dark: Whiteness and the Literary Imagination*. Cambridge: Harvard University Press.

Mulvey, Laura (1975/1989) 'Visual Pleasure and Narrative Cinema', in *Visual and Other Pleasures*. London: Macmillan.

Munro, Shaun (2012) '*God Bless America* Review: Irreverent and Bold Social Satire', *Whatculture!* 4 July, accessed online 5 November 2012 at http://whatculture.com/film/god-bless-america-review-irreverent-and-bold-social-satire.php.

Neale, Steve (1983) 'Masculinity as Spectacle: Reflections on Men and Mainstream Cinema,' *Screen* 24:6, pp. 2–16.

Nussbaum, Emily (2012) 'Child's Play: "Breaking Bad's Bad Dad"', *New Yorker,* 27 August, pp. 82–83.

Park, Jeana H. (1993) 'Does D-Fens Shatter American Reality or Reflect It?: Portrayal of Store Owner Seen as Volatile Stereotype', *Los Angeles Times*, 22 March, accessed online 27 August 2012 at http://articles.latimes.com/1993–03–22/entertainment/ca-13889_1_korean-american-community.

Parker, John (2011) *Michael Douglas: Acting on Instinct*. London: Headline.

Peberdy, Donna (2011) *Masculinity and Film Performance: 'Male Angst' in Contemporary American Cinema*. Basingstoke: Palgrave Macmillan.

Peretz, Evgenia (2010) 'Michael Douglas, Take Two', *Vanity Fair*, April, accessed online 8 October 2012 at http://www.vanityfair.com/hollywood/features/2010/04/michael-douglas-201004.

Pfeil, Fred (1995) *White Guys: Studies in Post-Modern Domination and Difference*. London: Verso.

Pulaski, Steve (2012) *God Bless America* nd, accessed online 5 November 2012 at http://stevethemovieman.proboards.com/index.cgi?action=display&board=reviews&thread=3104&page=1.

Rainer, Peter (1993) 'Falling Down Trips Over Its Own Hate: Movies: The Film Isn't Some All-Purpose Cry of Disgust. It's the Howl of a Scared, White, Urban Middle-Class Man', *Los Angeles Times* 15 March, accessed online 27 August 2012 at http://articles.latimes.com/1993–03–15/entertainment/ca-391_1_urban-middle-class.

Rauzi, Robin (1993) 'Box Office: ARE WE Falling Apart?: In its Third Big Week at the Box Office, "Falling Down" has Clearly Touched a Nerve. L.A. Moviegoers Tell Us Why,' *Los Angeles Times,* 15 March, accessed online 22 August 2013 at http://articles.latimes.com/1993–03–15/entertainment/ca-388_1_box-office.

Reeves, Richard (1993) 'Los Angeles is Falling and It Can't Get Up', *Seattle Times,* 18 March, accessed online 22 August 2013 at http://community.seattletimes.nwsource.com/archive/?date=19930318&slug=1691115.

Reinhold, Robert (1993) 'Horror for Hollywood: Film Hits a Nerve With Its Grim View of Hometown', *New York Times* 29 March, accessed online 29 July 2012 at http://www.nytimes.com/1993/03/29/us/horror-for-hollywood-film-hits-a-nerve-with-its-grim-view-of-hometown.html?pagewanted=all&src=pm.

Roediger, David R. (1994) *Towards the Abolition of Whiteness: Essays on Race, Politics, and Working Class History*. London: Verso.

Roediger, David R. (1999) *The Wages of Whiteness: Race and the Making of the American Working Class*. London: Verso.

Phillips, Kendall R. (2008) *Controversial Cinema: The Films That Outraged America*. Westport and London: Praeger.

Rhines, Jesse Algeron (1995) 'The Political Economy of Black Film', *Cineaste*, 21:3, pp. 38–39.

Rhines, Jesse Algeron (1996) *Black Film/White Money.* New Brunswick: Rutgers University Press.

Rosin, Hanna (2012) 'Flexible Woman and Cardboard Man' [excerpt from *The End of Men: And the Rise of Women*] *Observer: Review Section*, 1 October, pp. 8–11.

Salamon, Julie (1993) 'Film Review: *Falling Down*', *Wall Street Journal*, 25 February, p. A12.

Salisbury, Mark (1993) 'He's "An Ordinary Man at War with the Everyday World"…', *Empire*, July, pp. 76–78.

Segal, Lynne (1990) *Slow Motion: Changing Men, Changing Masculinities*. London: Virago.

Silverman, Kaja (1992) *Male Subjectivity at the Margins*. London and New York; Routledge.

Simkin, Stevie (2013) *Basic Instinct*. Basingstoke: Palgrave Macmillan.

Singal, Jesse (2007) 'The L.A. Riots: Fifteen Years After Rodney King: Key Figures: Soon Ja Du', *Time* accessed online 22 October 2012 at http://www.time.com/time/specials/2007/la_riot/article/0,28804,1614117_1614084_1614514,00.html   #ixzz2A2b-Vsv37.

Siske, Gene (1993) 'Film Review: *Falling Down*', *Chicago Tribune*, 26 February, C1.

Schumacher, Joel (1993/2009) *Falling Down* [Blu-ray disc].

Shaffer, RL (2012) 'God Bless America – Blu Ray Review', IGN, 3 July, accessed online 5 November 2012 at http://uk.ign.com/articles/2012/07/03/god-bless-america-Blu-ray-review.

Slotkin, Richard (1992) Gunfighter Nation: The Myth of the Frontier in Twentieth-Century America. New York: Atheneum.

Snead, James (1994) Colin MacCabe and Cornel West, (eds), White Screens/Black Images: Hollywood from the Dark Side. London and New York: Routledge.

Smith, Ebbe Roe (2012) 'Interview with Falling Down Screenwriter', accessed online 24 September 2012 at http://fallingdownfilm.com.

Sollors, Werner (1986) Beyond Ethnicity: Consent and Descent in American Culture. New York and Oxford: OUP.

Solomons, Jason (2012) 'God Bless America – Review', The Observer, 8 July, accessed online 5 November 2012 at http://www.guardian.co.uk/film/2012/jul/08/god-bless-america-review-bobcat.

Talbot, Margaret (2012) 'The Screen Test: How My Father Came to Act Alongside Stanwyck, Davis, and Lombard', New Yorker, 1 October, pp. 32–37.

Townsend, Mark and David Smith (2007) 'Return of the screen vigilante: Director Spotlights the Fate of Crime Victims and Iraq Veterans', Observer, 25 February, accessed online 5 November 2012 at http://www.guardian.co.uk/uk/2007/feb/25/film.filmnews.

Traube, Elizabeth G. (1992) Dreaming Identities: Class, Gender, and Generation in 1980s Film. Boulder and Oxford: Westview Press, 1992.

Trilling, Lionel (1940/1950) 'Reality in America', in The Liberal Imagination. New York: Viking.

Turan, Kenneth (1993) 'Movie Reviews: Everyman Can't Keep From "Falling Down"', Los Angeles Times, 26 February, Calendar, p. 1.

Vera, Hernán and Andrew Gordon (2003) Screen Saviors: Hollywood Fictions of Whiteness. Lanham: Rowman and Littlefield.

Ware, Vron (1999) 'A Room with a View', in Brown, Gilkes, and Kaloski-Naylor, White?Women, pp. 201–26.

Weinraub, Bernard (1992) 'The Talk of Hollywood: One Man's Riot Exploding from the Inside Out', *New York Times*, 9 June, accessed online 29 July 2012 at http://www.nytimes.com/1992/06/09/movies/the-talk-of-hollywood-a-movie-of-one-man-s-riot-exploding-from-the-inside-out.html?pagewanted=all&src=pm.

Weinstein, Philip M. (1992) *Faulkner's Subject: A Cosmos No One Owns*. Cambridge: CUP.

West, Cornel (1990) 'The New Cultural Politics of Difference', revised version in *The Cornel West Reader*. New York: Basic Books, 1999, pp. 119–139.

Willis, Sharon (1997) *High Contrast: Race and Gender in Contemporary Hollywood Film*. Durham: Duke University Press.

Woll, Allen L. and Randall M. Miller (1987) *Ethnic and Racial Images in American Film and Television: Historical Essays and Bibliography (Garland Reference Library of Social Science)*. New York: Garland.

Index